For Robbert and Floris,

the butter to my bread.

Tasty Tales is a uclanpublishing book

First published in Great Britain in 2024 by
uclanpublishing
University of Central Lancashire
Preston, PR1 2HE, UK

Text and illustrations copyright © Anna Lena Feunekes, 2024

978-1-915235-92-3

1 3 5 7 9 10 8 6 4 2

The right of Anna Lena Feunekes to be identified as the author
and illustrator of this work has been asserted in accordance
with the Copyright, Designs and Patents Act 1988.

All rights reserved. No part of this publication may be reproduced,
stored in a retrieval system, or transmitted in any form or by any means,
electronic, mechanical, photocopying, recording or otherwise,
without the prior permission of the publishers.

A CIP catalogue record for this book is available from the British Library.

Printed and bound in Great Britain by Page Bros Ltd.

anna lena feunekes

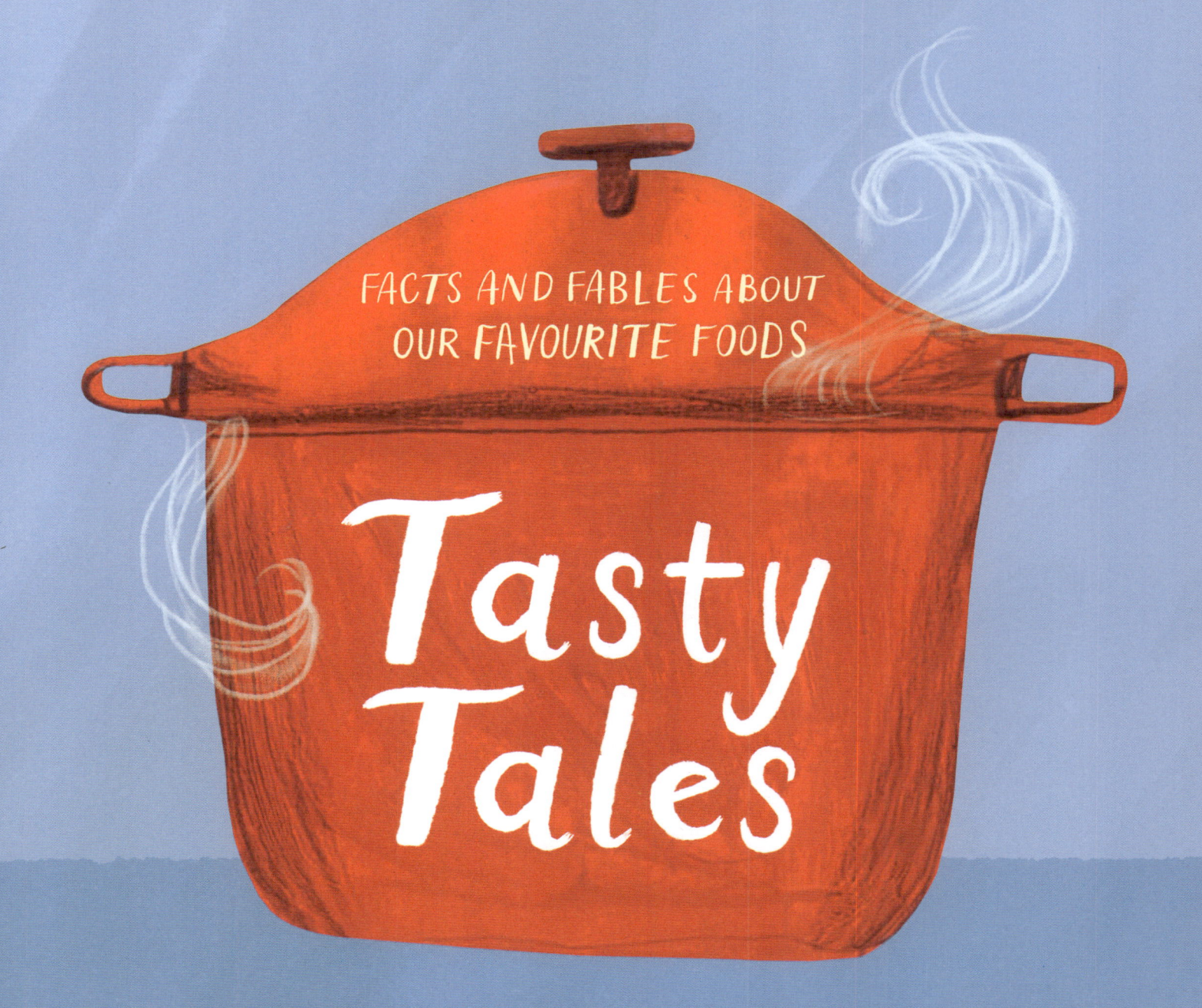

FACTS AND FABLES ABOUT OUR FAVOURITE FOODS

Tasty Tales

uclanpublishing

CONTENTS

- Introduction — 7
- Map — 8–9
- How the Croissant Got Its Curve — 10–12
- Why a Sweet Reward Helped to Build the Taj Mahal — 13–17
- Why Tomatoes Were Once Scary — 18–20
- Who Inspired the Pizza Margherita — 21–23
- How a Sleepy Sister Created the Tarte Tatin — 24–25
- How Om Ali's Sweet Revenge Became a Dessert — 26–28
- Why Pad Thai Noodles Are of National Importance — 29–31
- How a Plant-Loving Pirate Made England Cuckoo for Cocoa — 32–34
- When Ethiopian Goats Discovered Coffee — 35–37
- How a General's Maid Cooked Dulce de Leche — 38–40
- Why Okra Connects Cultures Across Oceans — 41–43
- Why a Chinese Granny Became a Tofu Trailblazer — 44–46
- How Potatoes Went From Poisonous to Prized — 47–49
- How Portuguese Sailors Inspired Tempura Shrimp — 50–53
- How a Lazy Earl Named the Sandwich — 54–56
- When a Sea Captain Gave the Doughnut Its Hole — 57–59

- How Ignacio Invented Nachos — 60–61
- When a Town Began to Race With Pancakes — 62–64
- Why Heri Heri Is a Symbol of Freedom and Cultural Heritage — 65–67
- How a Fairy Tale Inspired Gingerbread Houses — 68–71
- When Candyfloss Was a Banquet Dish — 72–74
- How Ramen Noodled Its Way Through History — 75–77
- When French Toast Was a Treat for Poor Knights — 78–80
- How Tea Became a Time of Day — 81–83
- Why Jollof Rice Is the Pride of West Africa — 84–86
- Why Ice Cream Cones Are Better for Us Than Penny Licks — 87–89
- Why There Is a Pineapple House in Scotland — 90–93
- When a Sneaky Sausage Saved Jewish People in Portugal — 94–97
- How a Mustard Army Spiced Up Dijon's Image — 98–101
- When a Mash Became a Symbol for Victory — 102–105
- Author's Note — 106–108
- Using the Recipes — 109
- Bibliography: The Recipe for this Book — 110
- Acknowledgements — 111

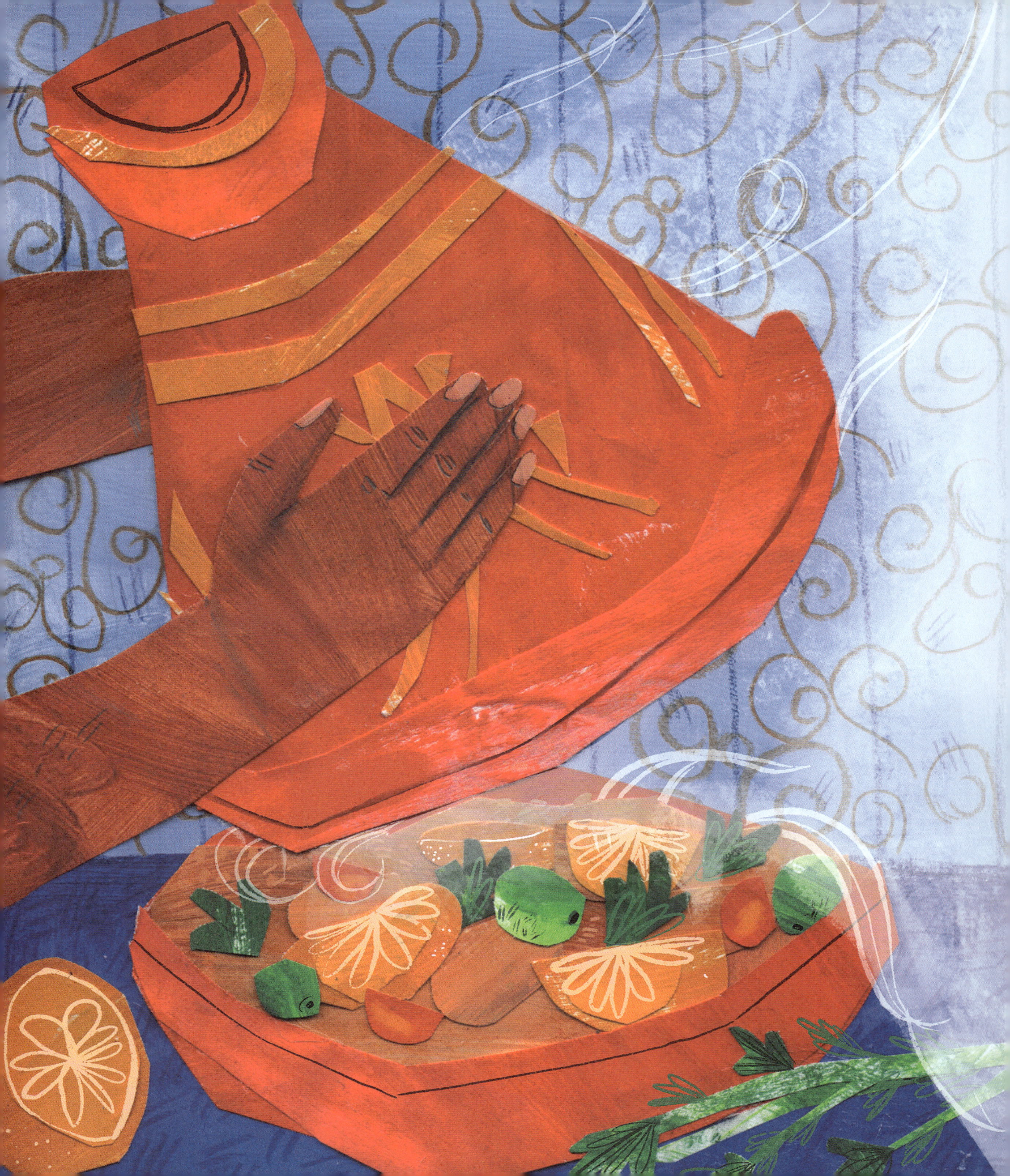

INTRODUCTION

In these pages, you will learn about a few of our favourite foods and how they came to be. You might also find dishes or places you've never heard about. Some foods were discovered by accident, others were made to bring honour, or to show resistance. A number of the stories are based on real history, while others are probably more like legends, as we cannot be sure if they really happened.

One thing that all the food in this book has in common is that it brought people together and let them express who they are: much like we do in the here and now when we sit down together for dinner.

Get ready to feast on some amazing stories!

Anna Lena Feunekes

Wij hebben nu nog slechts
vrouw Milligan voort; ik
Fransche
eenig

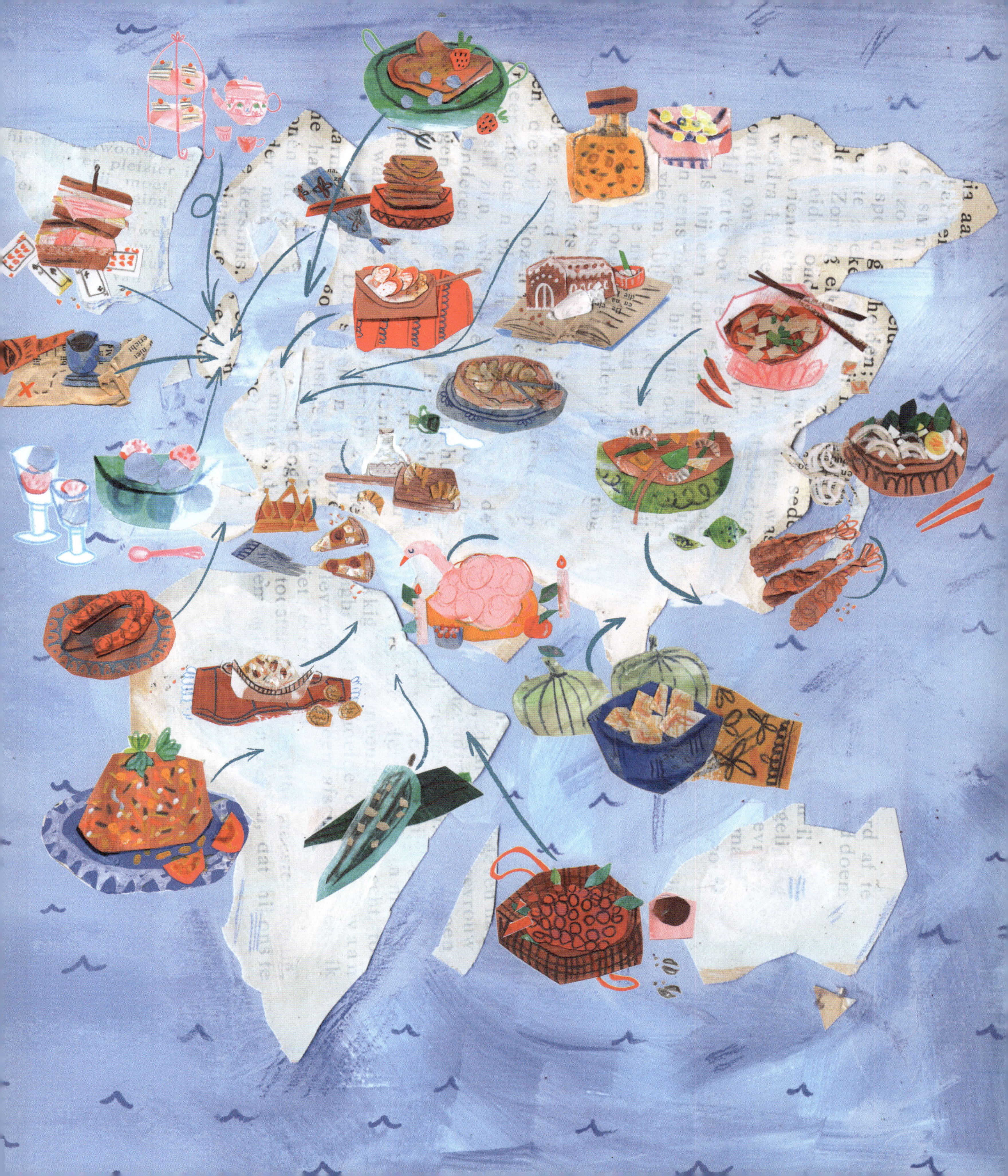

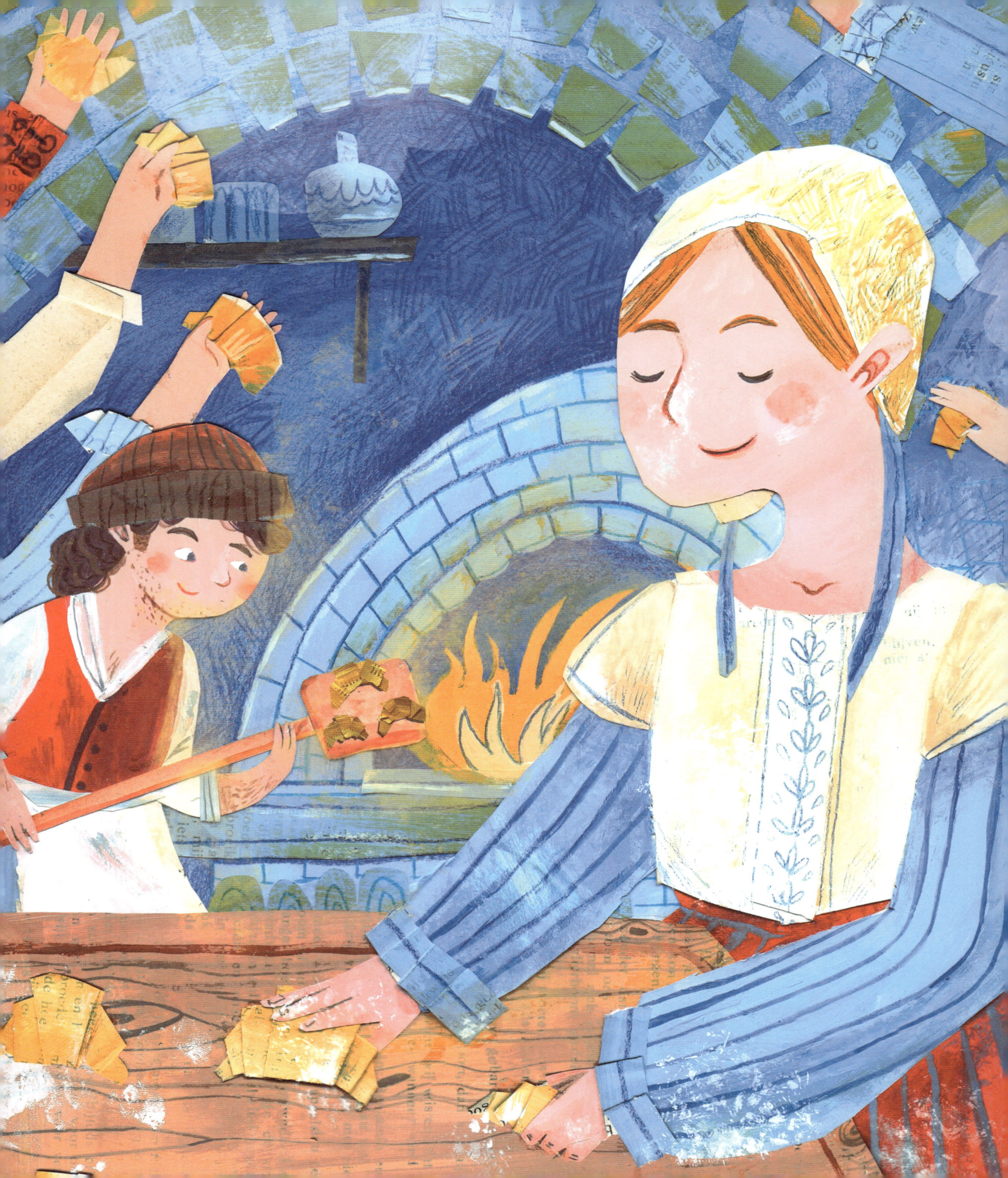

HOW THE CROISSANT GOT ITS CURVE

If you have ever eaten a croissant, you probably know that they are curved. But do you also know they are that way because they are shaped like the moon? The crescent moon, to be precise . . .

Croissants are rumoured to have first appeared in Austria after the siege of Vienna in 1683. Bakers woke up earlier than anyone else to produce the day's fresh bread, and one morning a baker heard strange noises, like someone was digging underground. The bakers discovered Vienna was being invaded by the army of the Ottoman Empire, which was once so large it spanned countries from Algeria and Bosnia to Egypt and Iraq. The bakers sounded the alarm, which meant the invading army was caught.

To celebrate their clever discovery of the Ottoman army, the bakers created a pastry shaped like the crescent moon they saw on the invaders' banners.

Next time you have a croissant for breakfast, remember: you're eating a pastry that is more or less symbolic of two proud nations!

WHY A SWEET REWARD HELPED TO BUILD THE TAJ MAHAL

Have you heard of the magnificent Taj Mahal, located in the city of Agra, India? This architectural wonder was commissioned by Shah Jahan, the ruler of that time, as a memorial for his beloved wife. Today, it attracts visitors from all around the world who come to marvel at its exquisite beauty.

But how does this iconic building have a connection to food?

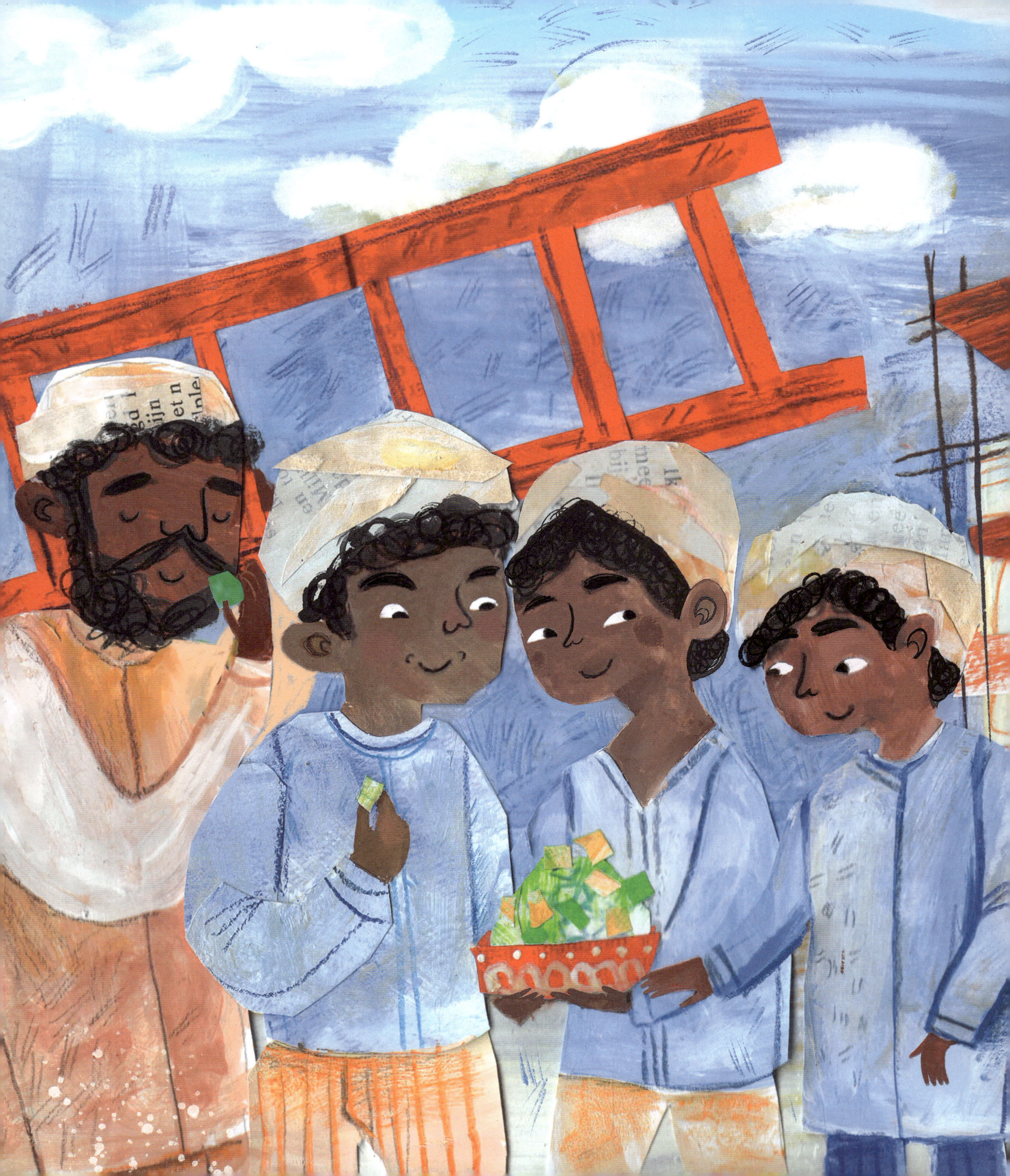

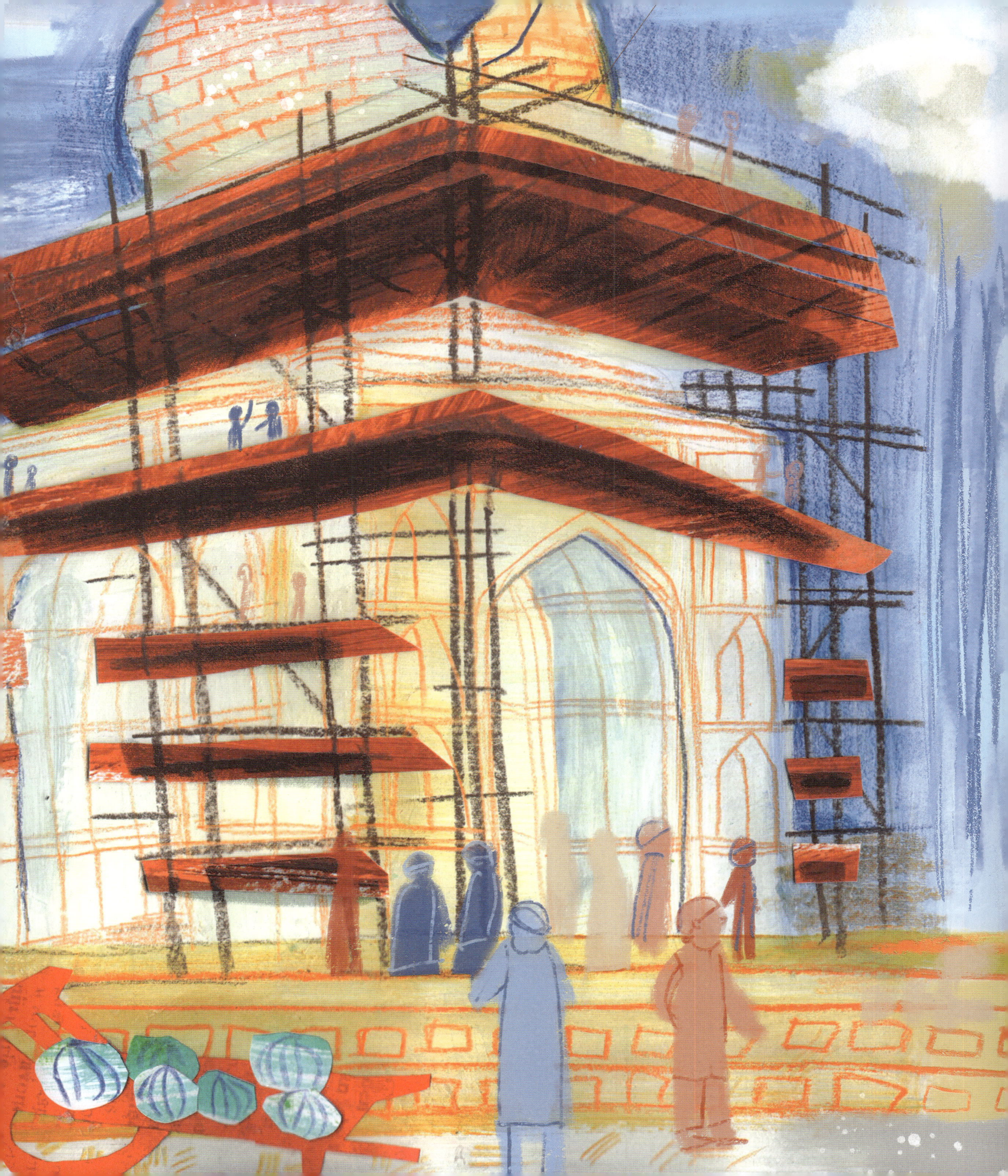

During the construction of the Taj Mahal, an interesting incident occurred. The dedicated builders, who had been tirelessly working on the project for a long time, began to feel demoralised. They ate the same simple fare every meal, and the repetition both in their work and their food, day in and day out, made them yearn for something different – something sweet.

In an effort to uplift their spirits and provide them with a burst of energy, Shah Jahan collaborated with his royal priest to create a delightful sugary treat. They used a specific variety of white pumpkin that grows in the Agra region and prepared the first ever batch of petha. To ensure an ample supply, around 500 cooks toiled throughout the night. Finally, the time came to distribute the treats and, needless to say, the workers were overjoyed to savour this special confection crafted especially for them.

Even today, when you visit Agra, you can taste petha, as it remains a popular local delicacy.

Renowned for its delightful sweetness, it has become an absolute must-try for visitors. Once a reward for builders' tireless efforts, petha has now become a beloved culinary tradition.

WHY TOMATOES WERE ONCE SCARY

A long time ago, some Spanish people travelled to America to find new land and collect objects and ideas they could take back to their own country. They found that the native people had a lot of interesting and valuable things, including a round, shiny and yummy fruit called a tomato. Before this time, people in Europe had never eaten a tomato, which is strange to think about because we eat tomatoes all the time now!

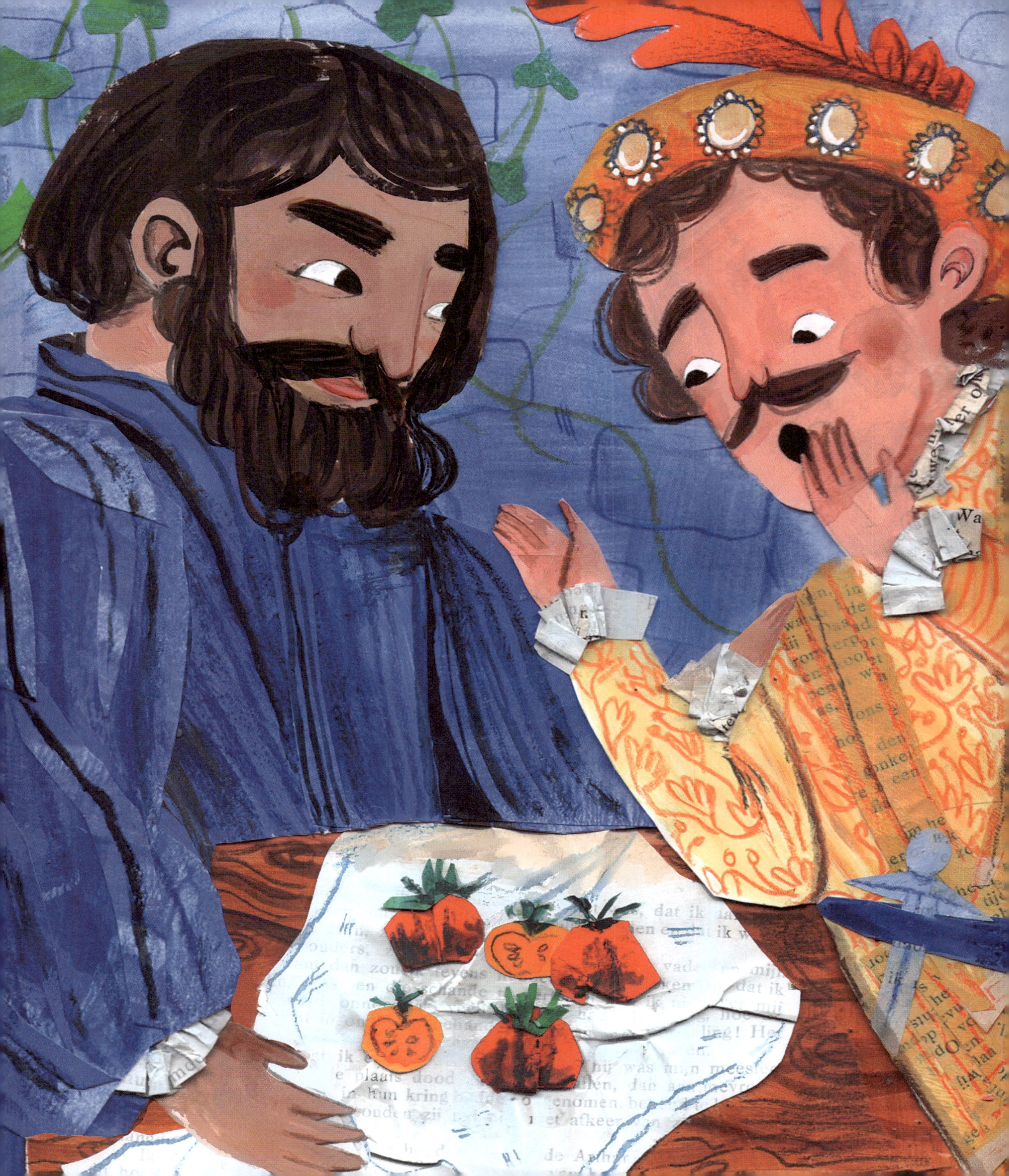

At first, many people in Europe thought the tomato might be a bad thing because they had never seen it before. They thought it might be the same as the fruit in the Bible story that caused Adam and Eve to be kicked out of the Garden of Eden. To make matters worse, after eating tomatoes from plates made of lead, some nobles even died! They didn't know that lead was very poisonous, and the acid in the tomatoes would soak up even more of the metal than they would normally consume at dinner. Yet, they blamed the tomato.

To make things even more mysterious, a man called Pietro Andrae Matthioli, who studied plants, thought the tomato was like a mandrake plant that people had been very scared of in the past. The mandrake looked like a person and so it was thought that the plant was dangerous and could hurt humans. Because of this, it took a long time before the tomato would be eaten by just anyone. Luckily, the introduction of the pizza and some of the other foods in this book helped a lot – and today, we can hardly eat anything without tomato in it!

HOW THE PIZZA MARGHERITA GOT ITS NAME

There is something humans everywhere have in common: we have been putting delicious toppings on flat bread for thousands of years. But there is supposedly something unique behind the Margherita pizza. You might know it as the first pizza listed on many menus – but how did someone come up with the name?

It is rumoured that in 1861, the King and Queen of Italy

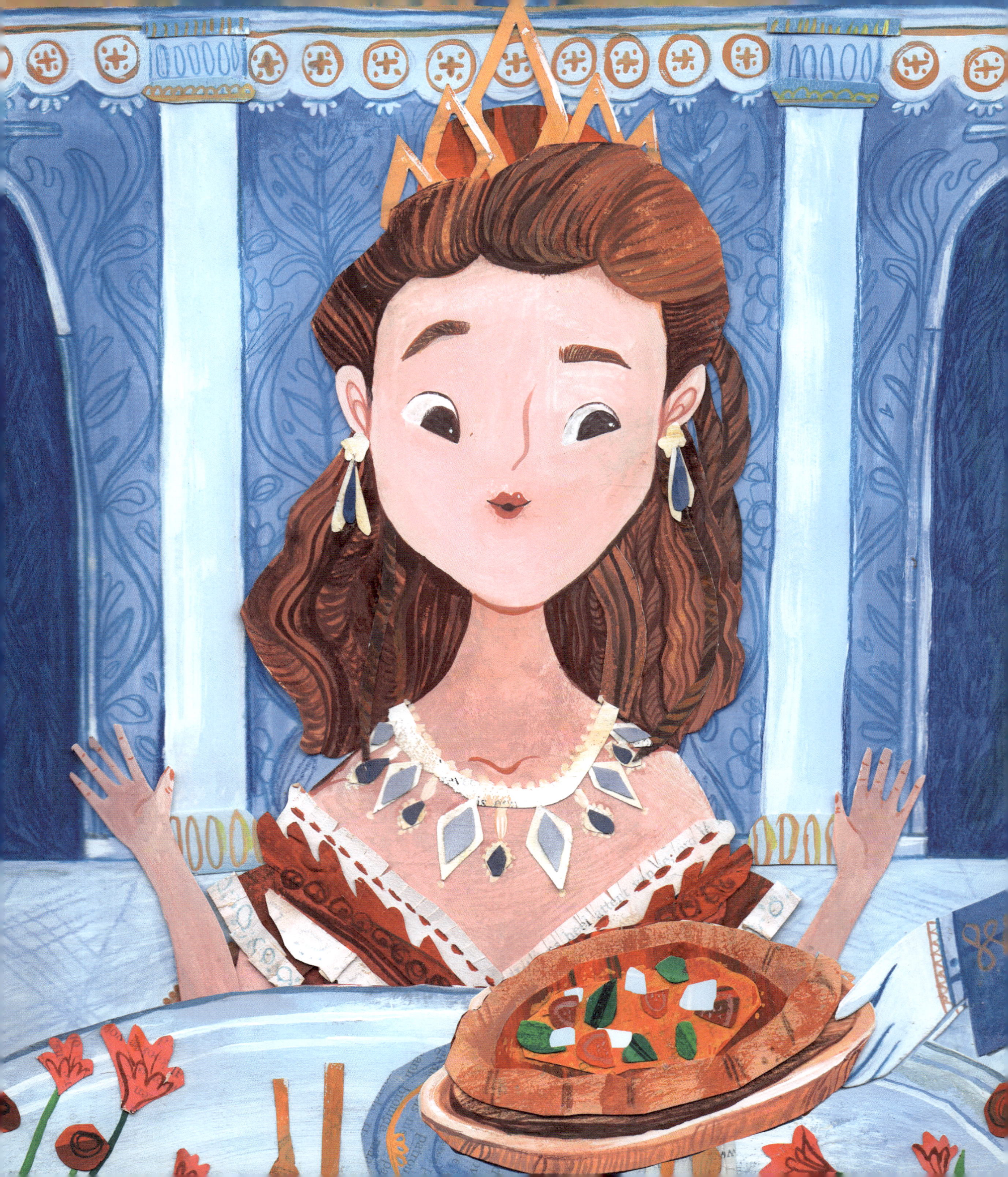

travelled to Naples to mark the official proclamation of the Kingdom of Italy. Before this date the Italy we know today was made up of several different smaller countries, but during 1861 agreements were made to unify them all into one country. In celebration, the royal couple paid a visit to this coastal city.

Local pizza chef, Raffaele Esposito, prepared a signature dish for Queen Margherita. It celebrated the colours of the national flag – green, white and red – with tomato, basil and mozzarella as the only ingredients.

The queen was delighted with the gesture and the taste! She expressed this to Raffaele, who then named his creation Pizza Margherita. That is how a pizza came to be named after a queen, and an ode to Italy's national colours.

HOW A SLEEPY SISTER CREATED THE TARTE TATIN

Long ago in a French town, there were two sisters named Caroline and Stéphanie Tatin. They lived in a cosy little bakery and loved to bake all sorts of sweet treats for the people in their town. One morning, Stéphanie was in the kitchen making an apple tart. She was in a hurry and accidentally put the apples in the pan before the sugar and butter. Caroline noticed the mistake and quickly turned the pan over to try and fix it.

To their surprise, the tart came out beautifully! The caramelised apples were on top and the crust was crispy and delicious. They called it the tarte tatin. The sisters began making the tarte tatin for their bakery and soon everyone in town was talking about it!

Word about the tarte tatin spread across France and people began coming from far and wide to taste this new and delicious dessert. Caroline and Stéphanie became famous for their invention and their bakery became a big success. Their mistake turned into a tasty treat that people still enjoy today.

HOW OM ALI'S SWEET REVENGE BECAME A DESSERT

Take a seat in any restaurant in Egypt and you will find a delicious dessert on the menu called Om Ali. It's made with puff pastry, nuts and cream, and it's very popular! But there is a legend about the dessert that's not so sweet...

A long time ago in Egypt, there was a woman named Shajar-Al-Durr. She was very special because even though she had been a servant, she married a king and became a

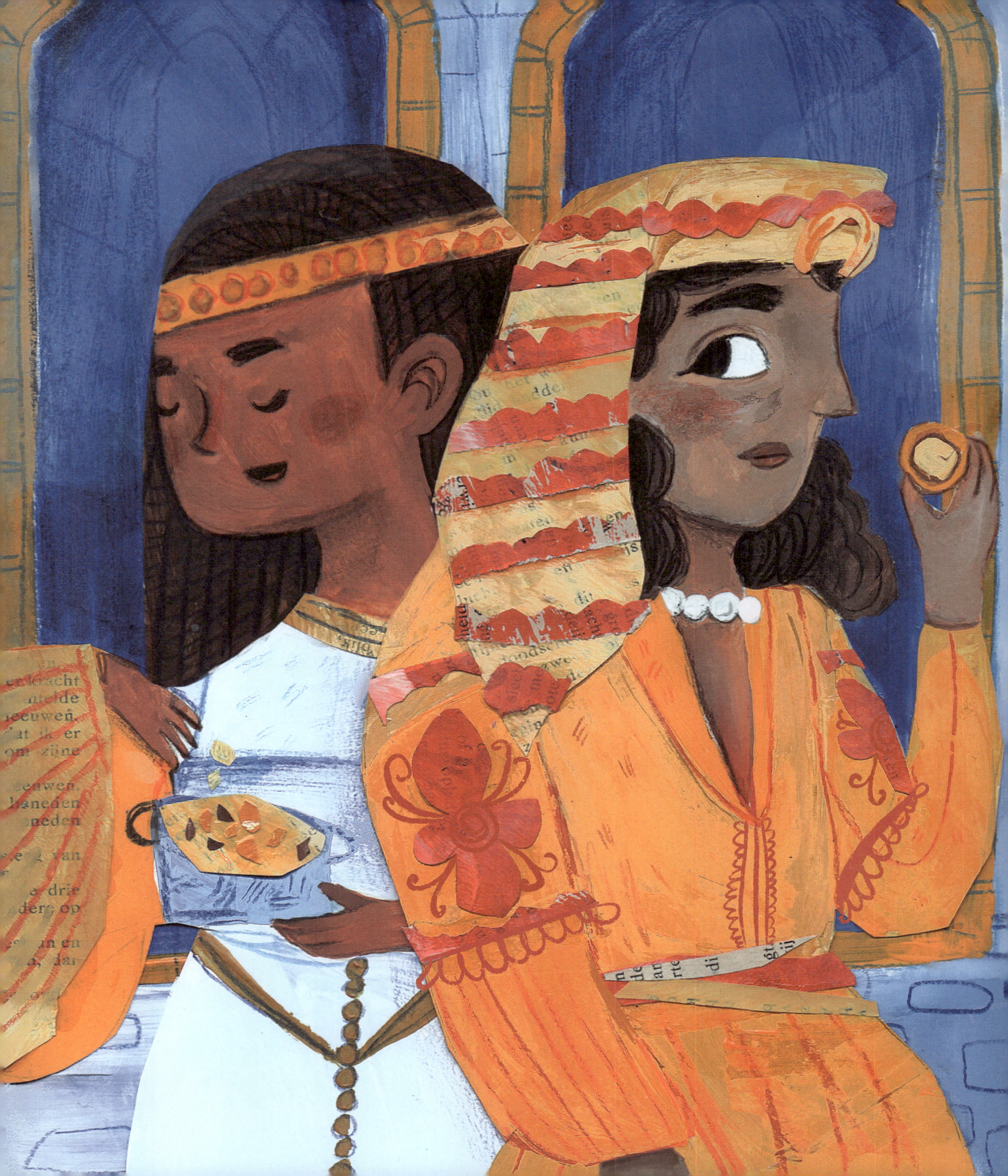

queen. When the king died, she became the ruler of Egypt! She even had her own coins made. Even though she was a good leader and won battles against invaders who wanted to take over Egypt, some of her own people didn't think a queen should rule alone.

To solve this, Shajar got married again to a man named Izz-Al-Din-Aybak. But he was already married to another woman, Om Ali, which Shajar didn't like. When Shajar then found out her new husband wanted to marry yet another woman, she had him killed in secret.

Om Ali, the first wife of Shajar's husband, was very smart. She worked out what had happened and wanted revenge, so she had Shajar put in a dungeon and then killed.

To celebrate her victory over Shajar, the first wife had a dessert made with one of Shajar's golden coins at the bottom of the dish. She named it after herself and her son, and that's how the dessert Om Ali got its name.

WHY PAD THAI NOODLES ARE OF NATIONAL IMPORTANCE

Right before the Second World War, which began in 1939, everyone in Thailand was worried about being taken over by other big countries like France, England and Japan. They had just become independent and wanted it to stay that way!

One political leader, Plaek Phibunsongkhram, who ended up becoming Prime Minister, had a plan to make Thailand proud and more united.

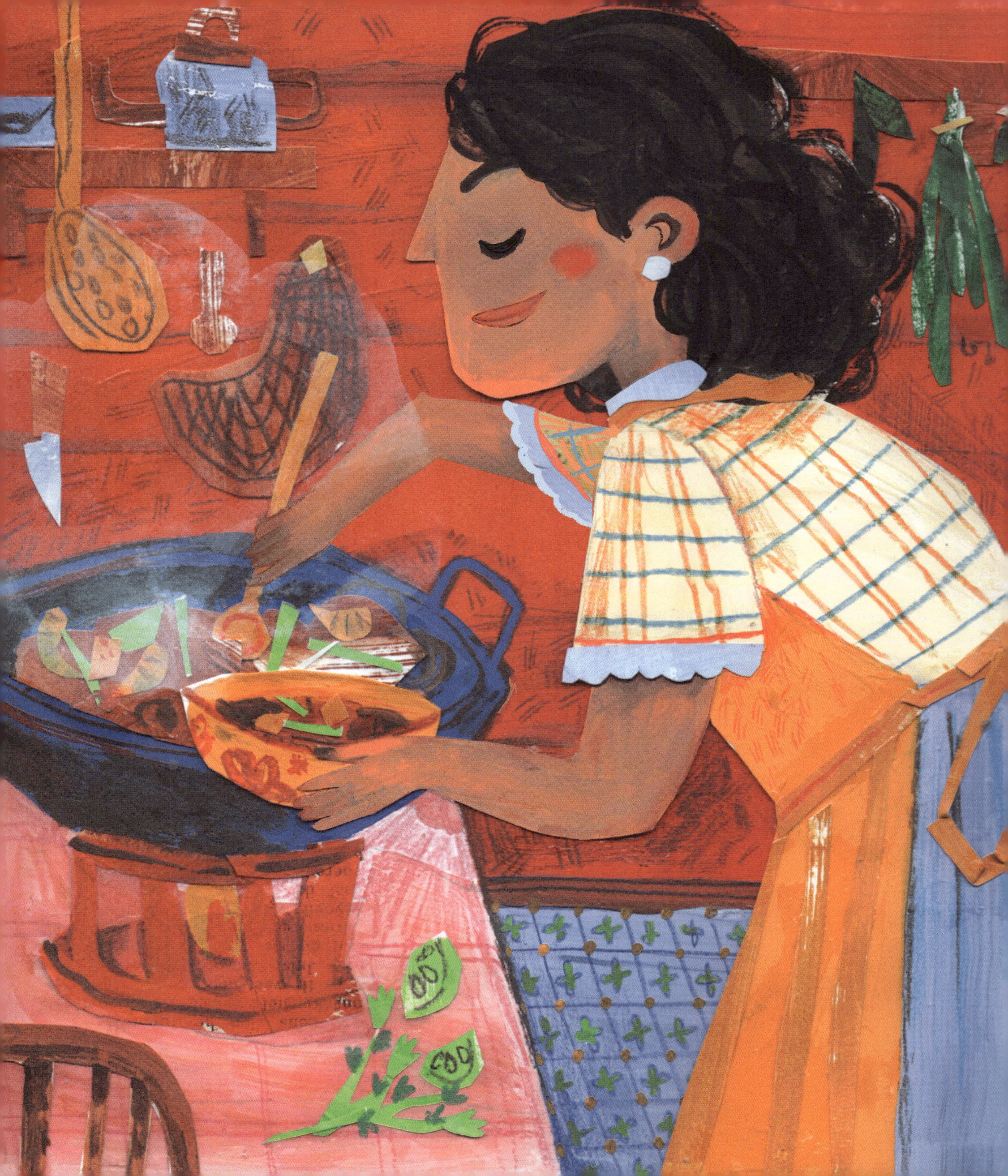

Phibunsongkhram believed that a strong national culture, including its food, was key to Thailand remaining independent. He made many changes to the country, such as changing its name from Siam to Thailand and dictating how Thais should dress, as well as stopping vendors of foreign food selling their wares.

Knowing that a national dish would help his cause, he decided to create one that would represent Thailand. He particularly liked a recipe that his housekeeper made, with rice noodles, egg, tofu, fish sauce, bean sprouts and lime, all particularly Thai ingredients. It was sweet, spicy and nutritious: perfect! Pad Thai became the national dish. The government even sponsored Pad Thai stalls and carts.

After the war, Phibunsongkhram was driven out of office and quite a lot of his changes were reverted, but Pad Thai stayed. Now it is enjoyed all over the world and seen as a classic Thai dish.

HOW A PLANT-LOVING PIRATE MADE ENGLAND CUCKOO FOR COCOA

Hot cocoa (you may know it as hot chocolate!) is made from the beans of a plant called cacao. The beans are ground up into a powder that are used to make delicious chocolate treats! Cacao was not something that people in Europe knew about until the Italian explorer Christopher Columbus made four voyages to the Americas in the 1490s and brought back the plant, along with other things like potatoes and tomatoes. These foods were already part of the diet of indigenous peoples of America, who used cacao beans to make a drink that Europeans thought was bitter and not very tasty.

That is until a pirate named William Hughes explored the Americas in the 1600s. He was a special kind of pirate called a privateer, which means he was working for the English government. Instead of stealing from the king, he was hired to make him richer. William was interested in plants and flowers, so when he tried the drink made from cacao, he wanted to learn more about it. By this point, Native Americans had begun to mix it with things like vanilla, honey and other plants to make it taste better.

Over time, Europeans got used to the taste. By the late 1600s, people in Spain and other parts of Europe were drinking cocoa all the time. But in England the favourite drink was still tea, which came from China. It wasn't until William Hughes wrote a book about his travels and the discoveries of peoples that he'd encountered, that cocoa became more popular in England. He called cocoa a 'nectar' which made it sound magical, and he was the first English person to write in the English language about the cacao plant. That caught everyone's attention . . . A long journey for a secret drink that took over the entire world!

WHEN ETHIOPIAN GOATS DISCOVERED COFFEE

There is a legend about a young goatherd called Kaldi, who lived with his goats in the highlands of Ethiopia. Kaldi spent most of his days herding his goats through the mountains, and one day, while out on his usual route, he noticed that his goats were acting quite strangely. They were jumping up and down! As he watched them closely, he realised that they were all eating the bright red berries from a certain tree. Curious, Kaldi decided to try some of the berries for himself, and he was sad to find that they had a bitter taste. Despite the taste, Kaldi felt a strange sense of energy and

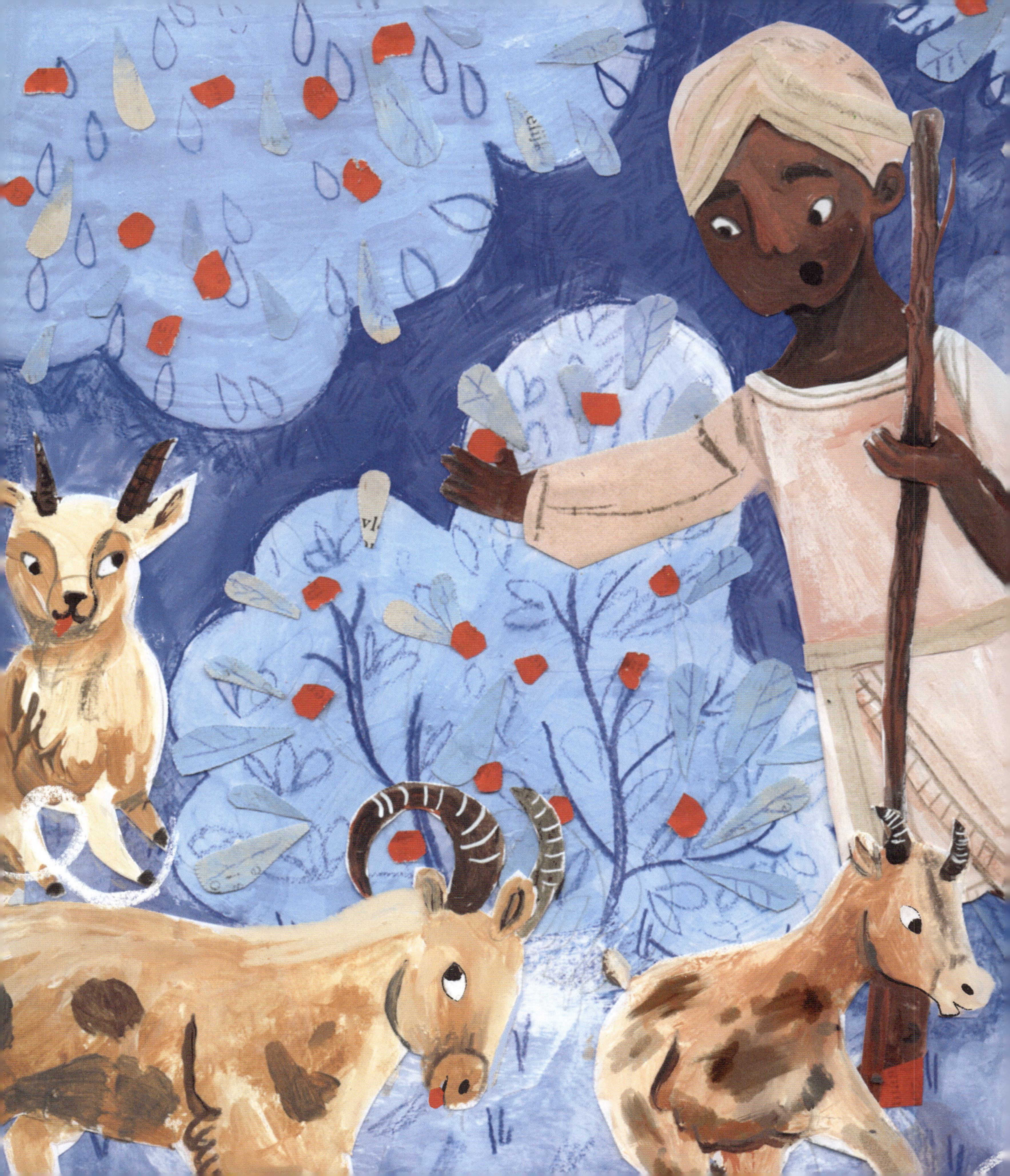

alertness after eating the berries . . . Intrigued, he gathered some of the berries and took them to a local monk, who tried to make a drink from them, but found the taste to be too bitter.

Undeterred, Kaldi continued to experiment with the berries, eventually roasting them over a fire and crushing them into a fine powder. He mixed the powder with hot water and found that the resulting drink was both restorative and energising. He had discovered what we now call coffee!

Word of Kaldi's brew quickly spread throughout the region, and soon people all over Ethiopia were drinking coffee. Eventually, the drink made its way to the Middle East, where it became a staple of daily life. And so, thanks to the curious young herder Kaldi and his goats, coffee became one of the world's most beloved beverages!

HOW A GENERAL'S MAID COOKED DULCE DE LECHE

In Argentina in the 19th century, there was a maid named Rosa who worked for an important man called Juan Manuel de Rosas. Juan Manuel was a powerful politician who was always busy with his work but was never too busy to eat desserts.

One day, Rosa was in the kitchen making some sweetened milk for her boss when she was called away to attend to another task. She left the milk to cool near the stove and forgot about it. When she returned, she found that the milk

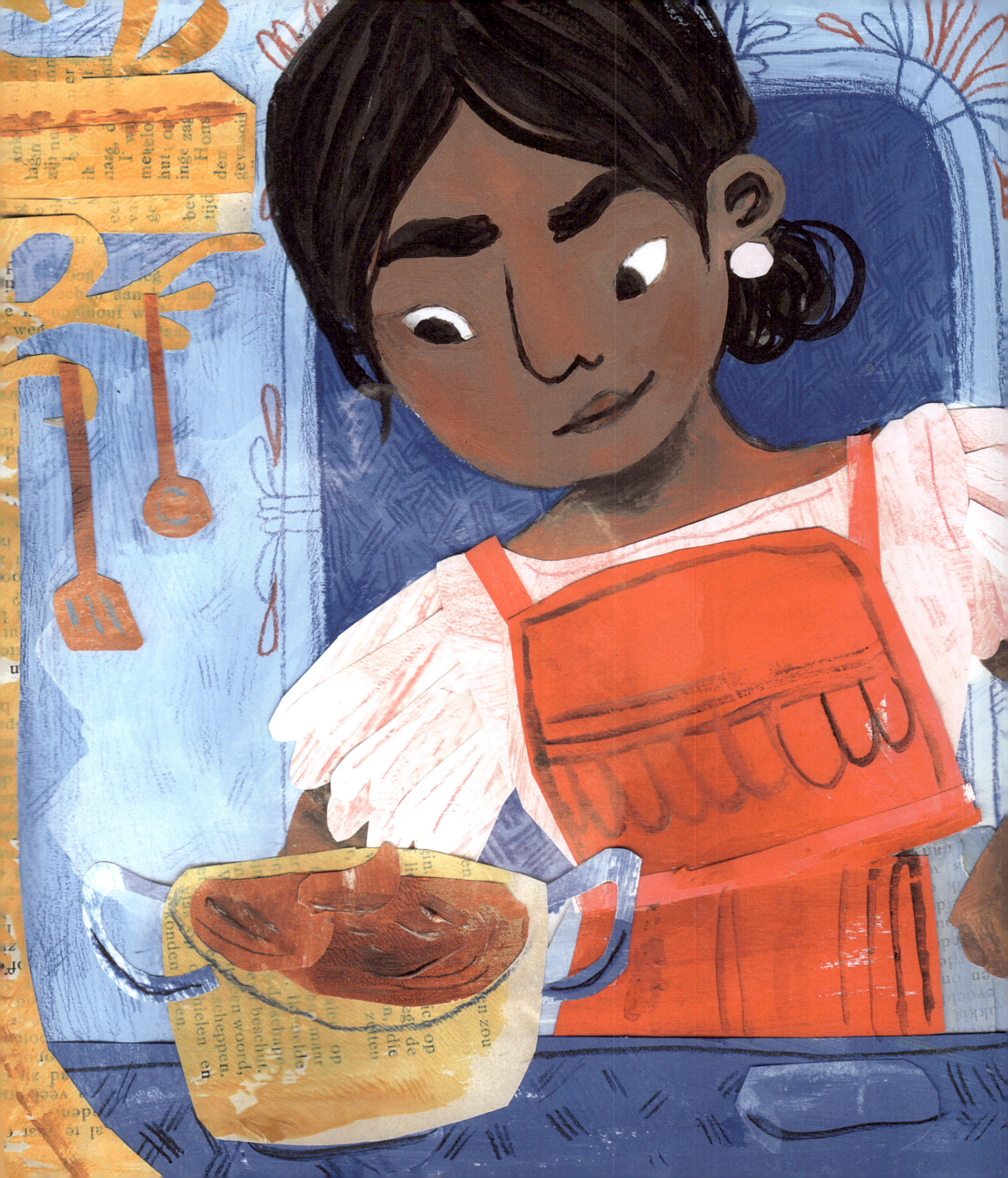

had thickened . . . When she tasted it, she discovered it was a delicious caramel-like substance!

Rosa served her newly discovered dessert to Juan Manuel that night. He loved the sweet taste and asked Rosa to cook it again. She knew then it would be a success and named it 'dulce de leche', which means 'sweet milk' in Spanish.

Word of this sweet treat quickly spread throughout Argentina, and soon everyone was making dulce de leche. It became a staple in Argentinean cuisine, used in everything from breakfast foods to cakes and desserts. And Rosa? She was so proud of her discovery that she never forgot to keep a watchful eye on the stove while making it, ever again!

WHY OKRA CONNECTS CULTURES ACROSS OCEANS

In the heart of West Africa, there is a much beloved plant known as okra. This fruit's journey across continents and its significance in food culture and history is a tale worth sharing!

Long ago, the people of West Africa discovered the virtues of okra. Some debate that okra had come from East Africa originally, from lands that are now part of Ethiopia, Sudan and Eritrea. The plant was taken on a journey to Egypt, Arabia and West Africa, where our story begins. With its vibrant green pods and unique flavour, it quickly became a beloved ingredient in West African cuisine. Okra thrived in the region's warm climate, and its versatility made it a staple in many traditional dishes.

During the transatlantic slave trade, millions of Africans were taken against their will to distant lands. Along with their own history and culture, they happened to bring seeds of their beloved okra. These resilient little seeds found their new home in the Americas, where they grew and became an essential part of life for many people. Okra helped connect people to their homes and ancestors, because even though life had changed so much, they could continue sharing their culture and making meals to stay strong.

Okra found its way into iconic dishes like gumbo, jambalaya, and pepper pot soup. In fact, gumbo is basically another word for okra: the plant that made it across an ocean became synonymous with a completely new dish! Gumbo is a stew made with okra, chicken, sausage and often seafood – a combination of African, Native American, French, Caribbean and Spanish cooking. Okra became a symbol and an essential ingredient that represents this fusion of cultures! Its influence reached beyond the kitchen, serving as a testament to the strength and enduring spirit of those who carried it across oceans and enriched culture in a foreign land.

WHY A CHINESE GRANNY BECAME A TOFU TRAILBLAZER

Mapo tofu is a dish made with tofu, minced meat and a special blend of spices. It's very popular in China today, and was created 150 years ago during the Qing Dynasty.

In the 1860s, a couple named Chen owned a small restaurant in Chengdu, in the province of Sichuan. Oil porters who crossed the nearby bridge would often stop at the Chen's restaurant and ask for a tasty meal.

陳太太豆腐

Mrs Chen had her own unique way of cooking tofu that looked, smelled and tasted amazing. She combined it with minced meat and her special blend of spices to create a dish that everyone loved. Mrs Chen's skin was marked after a bout of chicken pox, so local people called her 'mapo', which means 'pockmarked elderly woman'. So the dish became known as mapo tofu. When the Chen's restaurant became so popular, it was eventually renamed the Chen Mapo Tofu Restaurant.

By the late Qing Dynasty, Chen Mapo Tofu Restaurant was renowned as one of the most famous restaurants in Chengdu. People loved the flavour of mapo tofu, its affordable price, and how well it went with rice. As a result, it quickly became a staple of Chinese cuisine and can now be found all over the country.

HOW POTATOES WENT FROM POISONOUS TO PRIZED

When the potato was brought from the Americas, people in Europe didn't like it very much. In France, they thought it was poisonous and could make people sick – not realising potatoes were safe as long as they are not eaten raw! They even gave it to pigs instead of humans.

But a man named Antoine-Augustine Parmentier learned this was not true. When serving in the army he got captured and was forced to eat potatoes while imprisoned. To his surprise, he survived! After he was released from prison, he thought the potato could be a great food for France, because it was easy to farm.

Parmentier talked to important people in Paris and wrote an essay about the potato's benefits. He also hosted fancy dinners where he served lots of dishes made with potatoes. Guests at his dinners were said to include famous people like Benjamin Franklin, one of the Founding Fathers of America. Some say guests might have even brought the idea of french fries back to America. And even today there is a famous potato dish in Europe named 'parmentier'!

Parmentier didn't just stop at talking about potatoes. He is said to have planted a lot of them near Paris though he knew that hungry people would come and steal them. All of Parmentier's hard work paid off because everyone began to realise how good potatoes were as a food. They helped end hunger and became a staple crop in Europe.

However, the potato was not just good for eating . . . Marie Antoinette liked the flowers on the potato plant so much that she put them in her hair. Her husband, King Louis XVI, even wore one on his coat! This made the French nobles think it was fashionable to have potato plants on their clothes too. The next time you enjoy your french fries, think of the man who convinced everyone they were a good idea!

How Portuguese Sailors Inspired Tempura Shrimp

In the 16th century, Portuguese people faced a challenge. Their faith required them to not eat meat on certain days. They began to look for ways to work around this rule, while still satisfying their hunger, and created a dish of deep-fried, batter-dipped shrimp.

Portuguese fishermen traded with Japanese merchants and shared this recipe with them. The traders took it back home to Japan, where the dish was renamed 'tempura'. This Japanese name may have derived from the Portuguese word 'temporas', a reference to the Ember Days when meat was a no-go.

The Japanese quickly fell in love with tempura, which became a particularly popular snack food sold at street stalls. People ate it while standing and often used skewers to hold the morsels of fish, prawns and vegetables. By the beginning of the 19th century, tempura was sold in many places in Japan, and by the middle of the century, they were considered a delicacy among the higher social classes.

Today, tempura remains a beloved dish in Japan and around the world. Its crispy texture and delicate flavour make it a favourite among seafood lovers and foodies alike. All thanks to Portuguese fishermen and their quest to satisfy their hunger during days on which they couldn't eat meat!

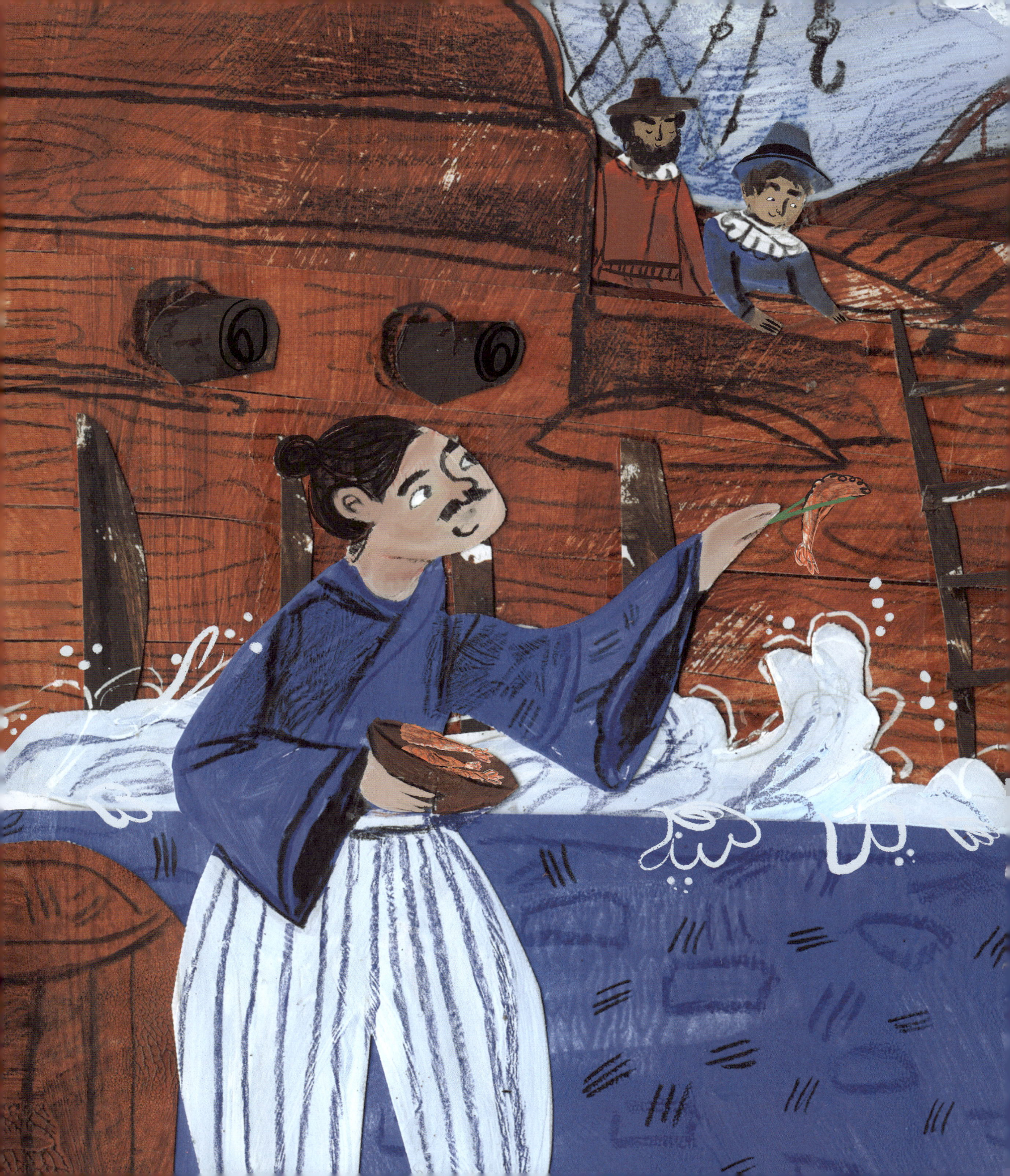

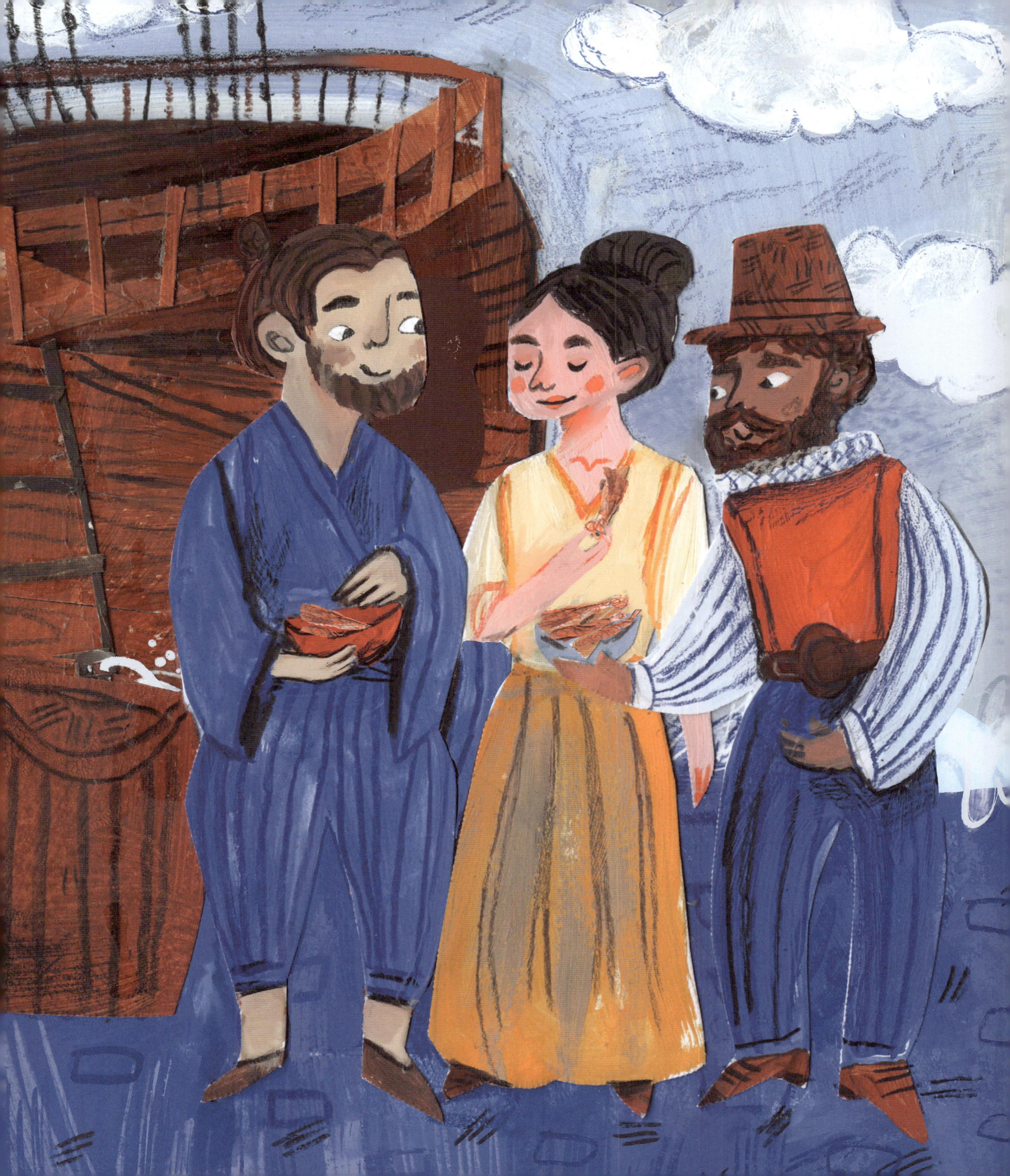

HOW A LAZY EARL NAMED THE SANDWICH

In England, there was once an earl named John Montagu, the fourth Earl of Sandwich, who is said to have brought us the name of the sandwich. The idea of eating meat and vegetables on bread was not new, but there certainly wasn't a name for it in his noble circles. If you were not as wealthy as him, you would have likely called it 'lunch' or 'bread'.

John Montagu lived in the 1700s, a time and a place where, if you were a rich person, eating dinner was something you didn't do quickly – or with your hands! But he was known as

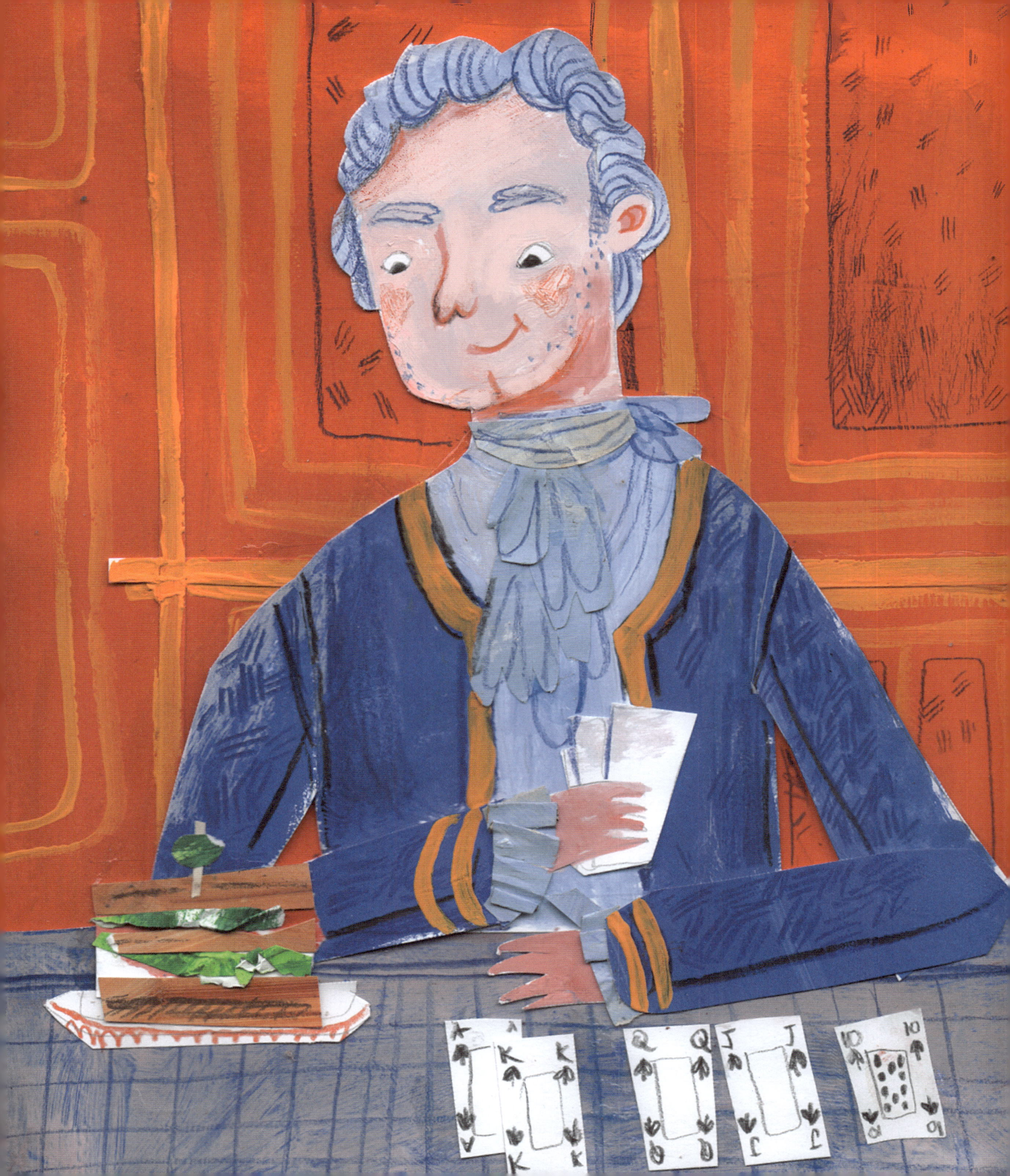

a lazy person who loved to gamble and didn't feel like doing much else, let alone stopping his game to eat.

The earl had seen people from Greece and Turkey eat pitta bread with their food, and thought it would be a good solution to his problem to do this at home. He sandwiched his dinner meat between bread and ate it on the go while finishing his game at the table. Though it was very inappropriate for someone from his rank, sandwiches became popular in England shortly after, even with fancy folk.

The sandwich appealed to rich and poor alike: it was easy to make, but also easy to make it look fancy. It could go with tea and a picnic, or could be a filling food after a night out. When trains were invented, the sandwiches on board were a handy thing to serve to passengers. And when people went to work, the sandwich was nothing more than a very old invention with a new name. The sandwich: named after an earl who just wanted to keep playing cards!

WHEN A SEA CAPTAIN GAVE THE DOUGHNUT ITS HOLE

Some credit the Maine sailor named Captain Hanson Gregory as the inventor of our beloved ring doughnuts. He would dream of doughnuts, imagining different flavours, shapes and sizes. In his time, doughnuts were round balls of dough that were fried in oil, without either the filling or the hole varieties we now have today. People from the Netherlands were the first to make these round 'nuts' of dough without holes, and brought them to New England in America.

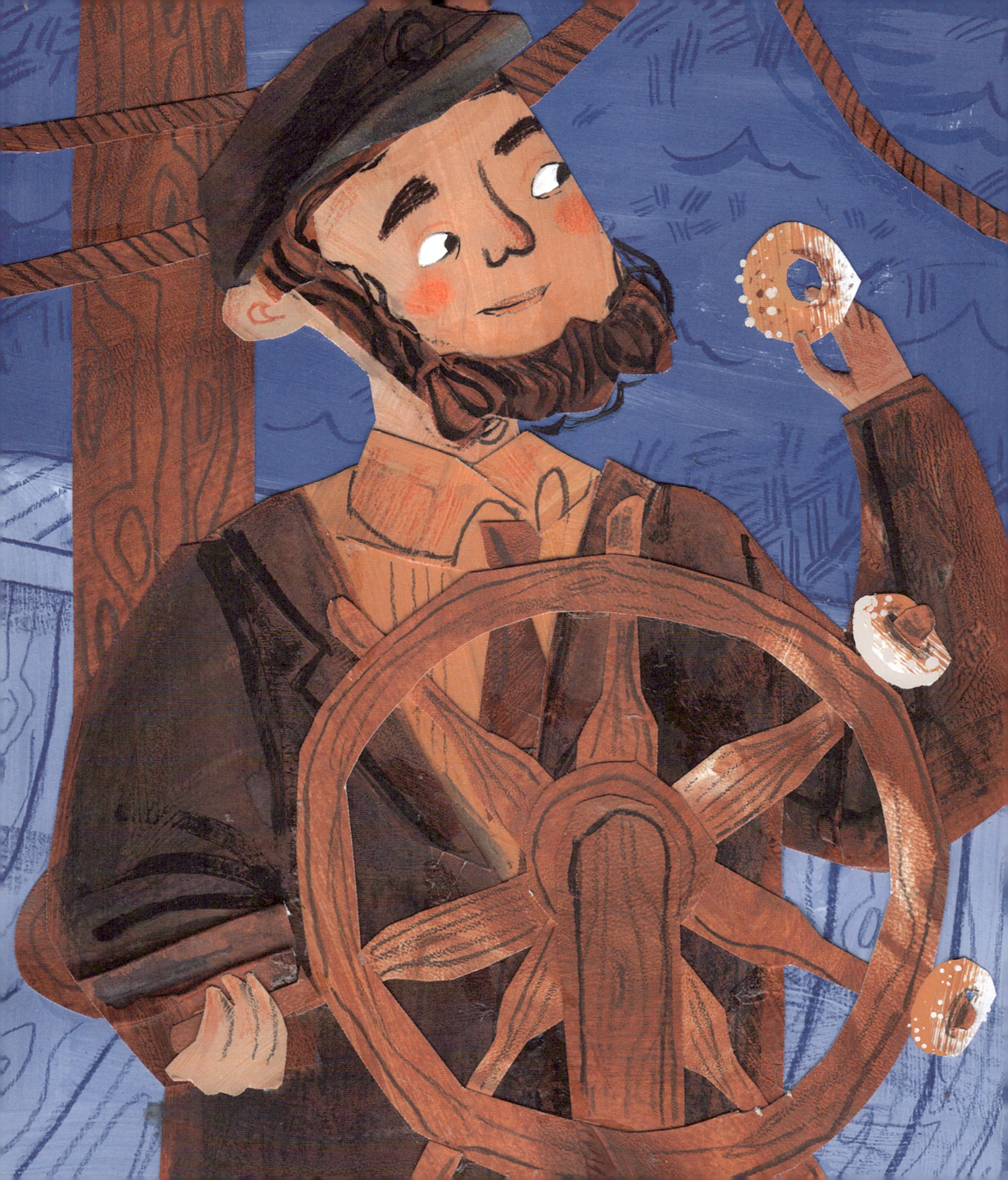

One day, Captain Gregory decided to make his own, but he found the dough too thick in the middle and too thin on the edges. Probably because he didn't know how to bake them very well . . . As he ate them, he realised that he only enjoyed the crunchy outer part, not the soggy middle. He wished there was a way to take out the middle bit of the doughnut and leave only the delicious outside.

And so, Captain Gregory took off the cover of the ship's tin pepper box and poked it through the centre of his doughnut, creating the first-ever doughnut with a hole! He was delighted and started making doughnuts with holes in the middle, which he shared with those around him.

So the next time you bite into a ring doughnut, remember Captain Gregory and how he changed the way we eat, and enjoy, doughnuts!

HOW IGNACIO INVENTED NACHOS

In 1943, at the old Moderno Restaurant in Piedas Negras in Mexico, waiter Ignacio Anaya invented a famous dish called nachos. When four guests asked for a snack, Ignacio got creative. With no one in the kitchen, he sliced a tortilla, added cheese and jalapeno, and baked it. The patrons loved it, and Ignacio named it 'Nachos Especial' – Nacho being a common nickname for Ignacio.

News of Ignacio's creation spread by word of mouth. He shared the recipe wherever he went – with extra pride, because he had been inspired by his own mother's quesadilla recipe! Today, nachos have many variations, but the original remains tortilla pieces, cheese and jalapeno pepper.

Ignacio could have made lots of money by patenting his creation, which would mean that only he could make it, but he chose not to. Instead, he opened his own restaurant and went on to raise a family. One of his sons carried on the family tradition by working at the new restaurant, and Ignacio remained happy about his invention, which is now served almost all over the world. Wherever Nachos Especial is served, his creation lives on, bringing joy to many.

WHEN A TOWN BEGAN TO RACE WITH PANCAKES

Humans have always loved pancakes! Even prehistoric people and the ancient romans used to eat them. There are many kinds of pancakes all over the world, with different ingredients and thicknesses and names: latkes, galettes, boxty, crêpe, drop scones, flapjacks, blini, poori, qata'if, dadar gulung, bao bing . . . take your pick! Some have sweet ingredients like fruit and nuts, while others are savoury, using potato, cheese or fish.

In medieval times, there is mention of a pancake much like

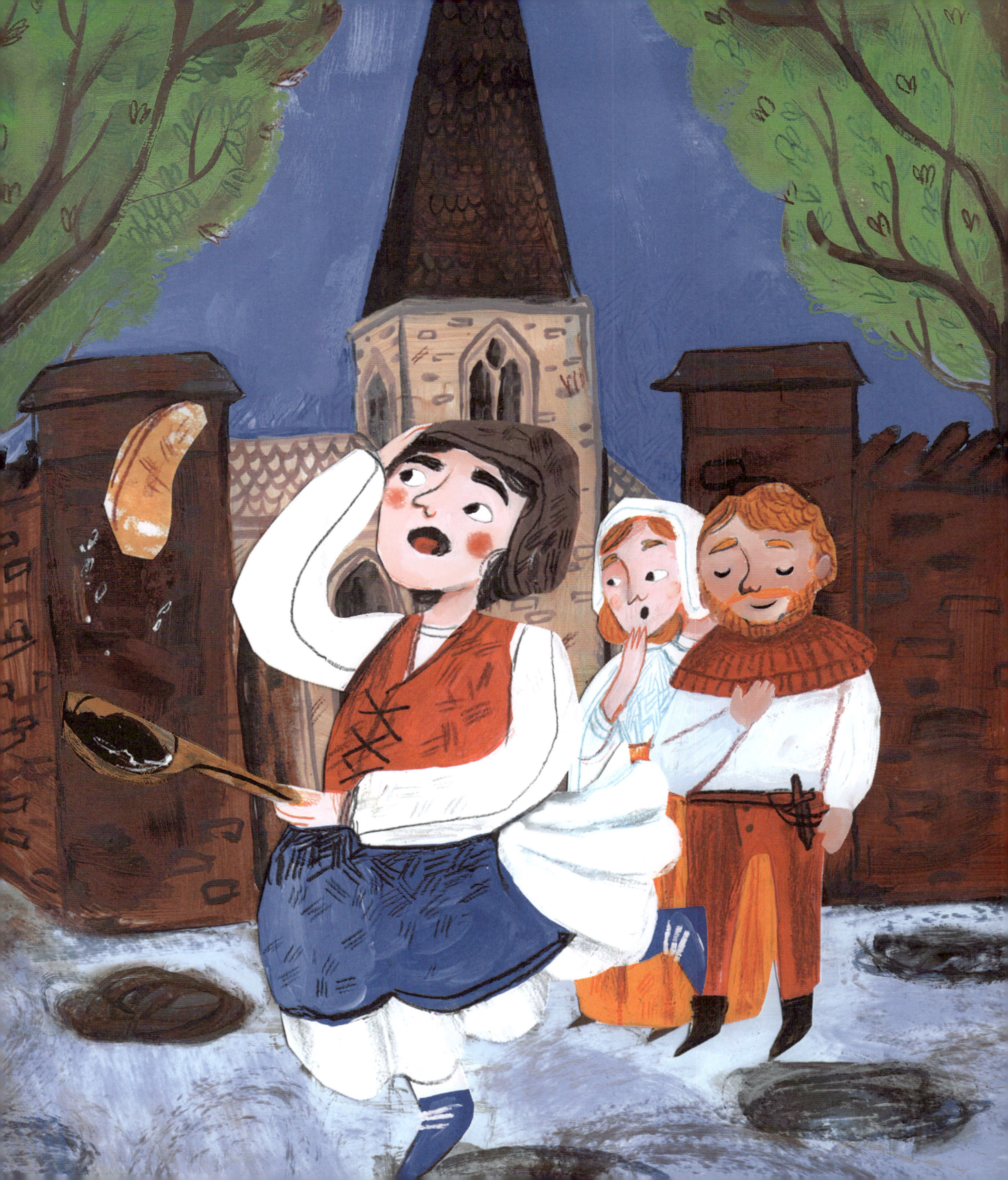

the one you know from today. People made pancakes around that time because they couldn't eat eggs and fats like butter during Lent, a Catholic tradition of fasting. Pancakes were an easy way to use up these ingredients beforehand. It's a tradition that still lives on today as pancake day (Shrove Tuesday) and Mardi Gras (which means Fat Tuesday). However, the surrounding tradition is odd. Have you ever heard of a pancake race?

Every year in a town called Olney in the United Kingdom, people run a race while holding a pan containing a hot pancake. Legend says that in 1445, an Olney woman heard the church bell toll while she was making pancakes and ran all the way to the church to see what was happening, still holding the pan with the pancake in it!

In the race, contestants even have to flip the pancake in the air while running! It makes you wonder if the woman did the same on her way to the church . . . But, lucky for us, we can eat pancakes without having to run for them!

WHY HERI HERI IS A SYMBOL OF FREEDOM AND CULTURAL HERITAGE

Heri heri is made from cassava, sweet potato, plantain and egg. It is often served with bakkeljauw, cod that is spiced with garlic, onion and hot madame jeanette chilli peppers.

Heri heri is a delicious dish, with a backstory that makes you think: it's a combination of foods that were given to enslaved peoples in the Caribbean that is today used for celebrations and to remember what has happened.

After roughly 400 years, the transatlantic slave trade ended. In Suriname, this was on 1 July in 1863. The Netherlands played a major role in the trade of human lives there until that time. This day is remembered as Keti Koti, but the term is used to describe the end of slavery in more lands that the Dutch controlled: Sint Eustatius, Saba, Aruba, Bonaire, Curaçao and Sint Maarten.

Although it might have been borne from slavery, people never stopped making and enjoying heri heri. Over time, the dish grew to be a notable part of the day of Keti Koti and an absolute delicacy. Heri heri is prepared for birthdays and celebrations and, because its ingredients are found in most Caribbean dishes, it is a symbol of unity.

Nowadays, on the day of Keti Koti, people all over the world eat heri heri! In 2023, an event called Free Heri Heri for All opened the doors of the Dutch Royal palace to 16 chefs with Afro-Caribbean roots, who prepared thousands of free portions of heri heri for people in Amsterdam. Because the wealth of the Netherlands has much to do with the slave trade, still visible in details of the Royal Palace, this event was powerful in its symbolism. What remained on the day of Keti Koti was remembrance, but mostly connection and celebration!

HOW A FAIRY TALE INSPIRED GINGERBREAD HOUSES

People have been making gingerbread for a long time, but the story of Hansel and Gretel from Germany might have started the tradition of making houses out of sweets! The story is about two children who find a house made of bread and sugar in the woods.

After 1812, when the story was published in a book of fairy tales by the Grimm brothers, German bakers began making

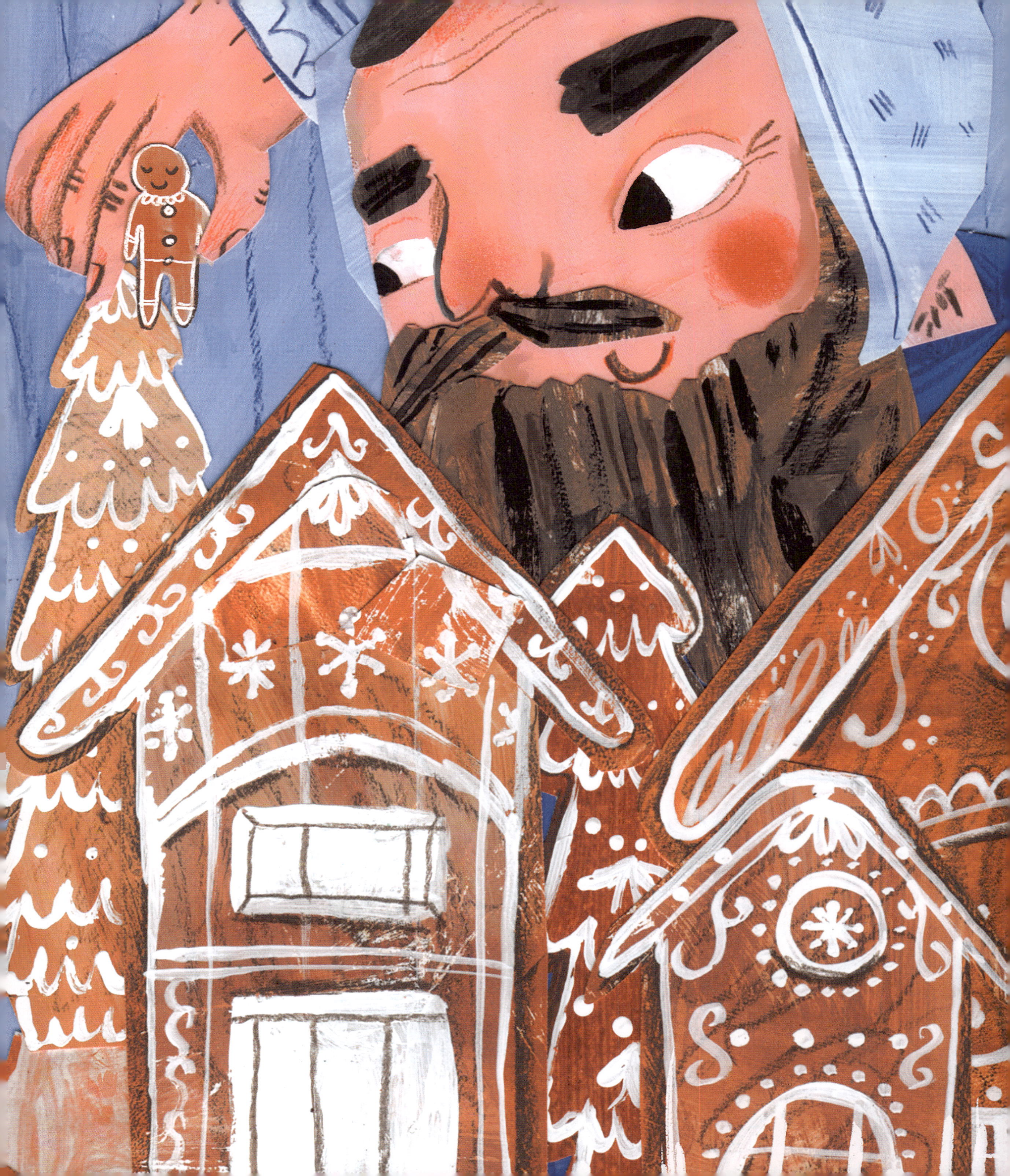

their own versions of the house using spiced biscuits. They were so pretty that they became especially popular during Christmas. The bakers who made these houses were important and respected. For some time, only they were allowed to make gingerbread in Europe. But they didn't just make houses, they sometimes also decorated them with gold leaf!

Gingerbread is an odd name for something that looks and tastes like biscuits. It got that name because the Old French word for it is 'gingerbras', which means 'preserved ginger'. Ginger was brought to Europe from the Middle East by the Crusaders, and it was tasty, spicy and sweet. Ginger is special as it also helped preserve bread and cakes. People started making gingerbread biscuits in Europe and then brought the tradition to America.

Gingerbread cookies became popular in America because they were cheap and easy to make. People would use wooden moulds to shape the cookies, like we use cookie cutters today. Bakers sold their gingerbread cookies at fairs and markets, and that's why we think of gingerbread as a festive treat. Thanks to the bakers and the ingredient's special powers, we get to enjoy beautiful and delicious gingerbread every December.

WHEN CANDYFLOSS WAS A BANQUET DISH

If you've ever been to a fair or theme park, you might have seen candy floss, or cotton candy as it's sometimes known – it's a fluffy, sugary treat that comes in lots of different colours. To make it, someone stands in front of a big machine with a spinning drum full of sugar, and they twirl a stick around inside the drum, picking up the melted sugar as they go. Within seconds, they've created a cloud of candy floss that you can carry around and eat.

Candy floss has actually been around for a long time. In the

18th century, fancy cooks and bakers in Europe and America would make it, but it was very expensive and hard to do. Chefs in Iran also created a version of it known as 'pashmak', which is often flavoured with sesame or cardamom.

Wherever it was made, the sugar first had to be melted, which became really hot and could be dangerous. Plus, it took a lot of practise to get the sugar nests to look just right . . .

Since only the fanciest guests could afford to eat it, the chefs sometimes got a little carried away. In the 16th century, the King of France went to Venice and was treated to a feast made entirely out of sugar! Even his cutlery was created from spun sugar. And in the 19th century, a famous chef called Marie-Antoine Carême created entire cities out of spun sugar, complete with windmills, temples and even gondolas.

But it wasn't until 1897 that someone invented a machine to make candy floss quickly and easily. Now you can find it in lots of places – and there are even small machines you can use at home! So next time you see someone twirling a stick around in a candy floss machine, you'll know the interesting history behind this sweet treat.

HOW RAMEN NOODLED ITS WAY THROUGH HISTORY

Have you ever eaten ramen noodles? They're a delicious soup of broth and noodles, with meat or vegetables and sometimes a boiled egg, which many people enjoy slurping up from a bowl. While most people think of ramen noodles as something that comes from Japan, they actually have their roots in China. They were originally called shina soba, which means 'Chinese soba', before becoming 'ramen', borrowing a word from Mandarin which means 'pulled noodles'.

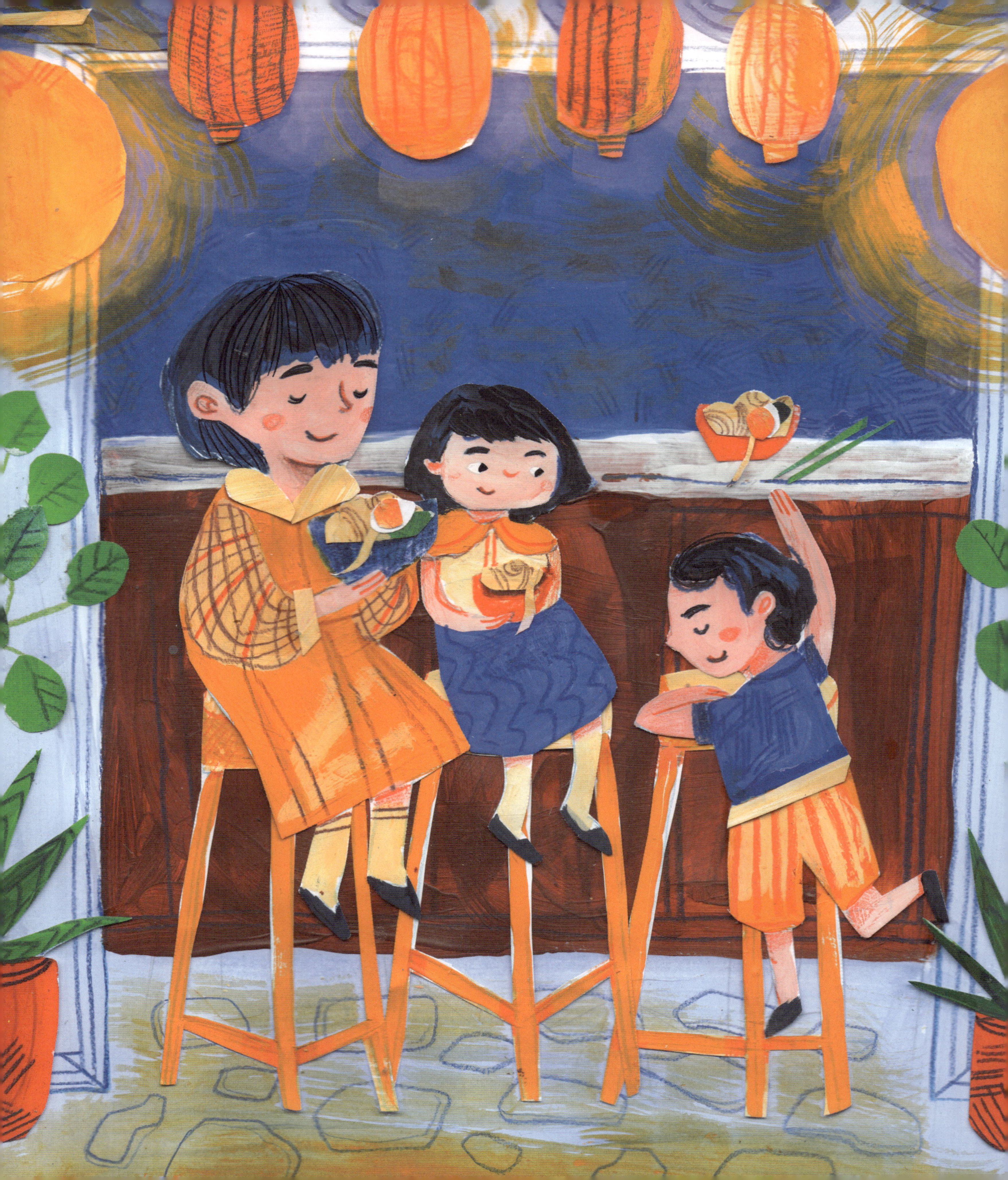

After the Second World War, which ended in 1945, many Japanese people who had lived in China opened ramen shops. Food was scarce in Japan at the time, and ramen was a nutritious dish that offered more protein than other traditional Japanese noodle dishes. Ramen shops have remained popular in Japan ever since.

In the 1950s, a man named Momofuku Ando realised that a quality, convenient ramen product would help to feed the masses. In 1958, he invented 'Chicken Ramen', the first instant ramen. Japanese grocery stores sold fresh Japanese noodles at a much lower price, but Mr Ando's new product made it easy to eat and serve them.

These days, instant ramen noodles are sold all over the world and are a popular and affordable meal. But freshly made ramen is popping up everywhere too, reminding everyone of the origins of Ramen as a food that was not just cheap, but also healthy, and deserves to be slurped!

WHEN FRENCH TOAST WAS A TREAT FOR POOR KNIGHTS

French toast, a fancy breakfast food today, was actually a humble dish for knights in medieval times. Before that, it was enjoyed by people all over Europe, tracing back to the ancient romans. The French had a funny name for it: 'Pain Perdu', which means 'lost bread'. They used to dip leftover hardened bread in milk to soften it up and cook it on a hot stove with butter or oil.

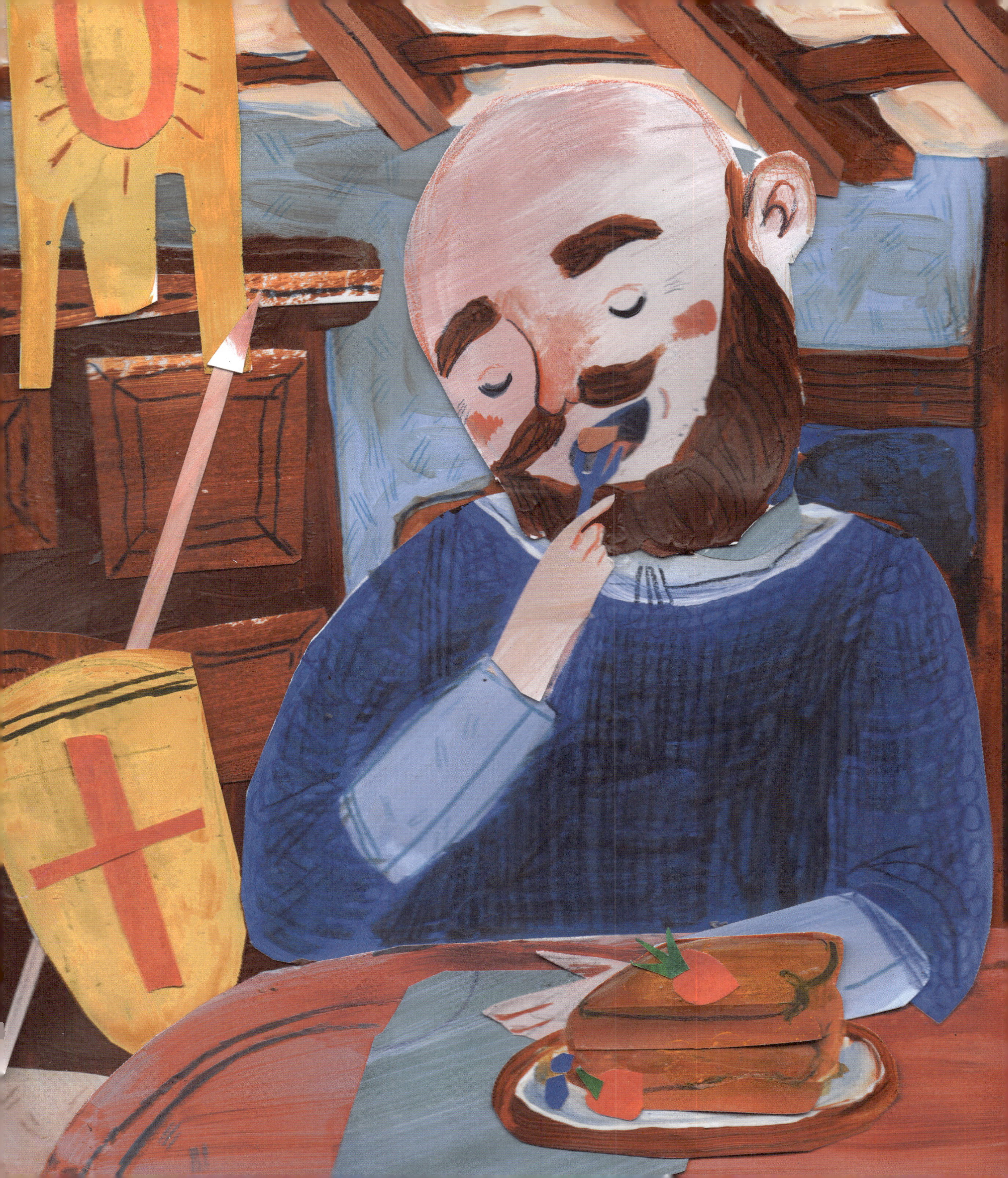

While poor people ate it too, the rich made it with white bread, which was expensive, and cut off the crusts. Medieval recipe books include methods that used white bread and expensive ingredients like spices and almond milk, but not many people could afford such luxuries or even had access to cookbooks.

Knights were usually commoners that served the nobles and couldn't afford to have fancy desserts made with expensive ingredients. To keep their social standing, they used leftover bread and cheaper ingredients to make desserts like french toast, which was then mockingly called 'armer ritter', meaning 'poor knight'.

Next time you sit down and enjoy a fancy french toast or some simple eggy bread, remember their sweet beginnings and how it was a clever way to use up leftover bread.

HOW TEA BECAME A TIME OF DAY

When we drink a cup of tea now, we don't really stop to think where it comes from. Some say that tea was discovered thousands of years ago by an emperor named Shen Nung, or Shennong. He loved to drink boiled water because he believed it kept him healthy. One day, as he was sitting under a tree, a leaf fell into his cup of hot water. Instead of being annoyed, he decided to drink it anyway and to his surprise, it tasted amazing!

At first, tea was only used for health purposes, but it

soon became so popular that people began trading it as a delicacy. First, the Chinese would only drink green tea, but when they started trading with other countries like Portugal, they needed to find a way to keep it fresh during long journeys. So, they tried fermenting and baking the tea, adding other herbs and plants, which created black tea and flower-scented tea. This helped to keep it flavourful, despite the long voyages by ship.

One day in 1662, a queen named Catherine of Braganza came to England from Portugal to marry Charles II, the King of England. She loved drinking tea and introduced it to the British. Soon, tea became very popular and people began drinking it in coffee houses. It was even smuggled because it was so valuable, with bandits trying to fool people by mixing green tea with clay and other plants so they could charge more. Black tea was harder to mix with things, which is why it may have become the most popular.

The final step was the invention of teatime. One clever duchess of Bedford named Anna Maria Russell decided in 1840 that tea was too good to be just a drink, so she invented afternoon teatime, making it a party! She invited her friends over for tea and cakes, and it soon became a tradition and a specific time of day. And that is how teatime was born.

WHY JOLLOF RICE IS THE PRIDE OF WEST AFRICA

Countries such as Senegal, Ghana and Nigeria all claim to be the birthplace of this delicious spicy rice dish. It is eaten in many places, with each country having their own unique twists and variations. The dish typically consists of broken rice cooked in a flavourful tomato-based sauce with spicy peppers, and it is often served with meat, fish, seafood or shito (a hot black pepper sauce), and a variety of vegetables, depending on who cooks it and where!

One theory suggests that jollof rice originated from the

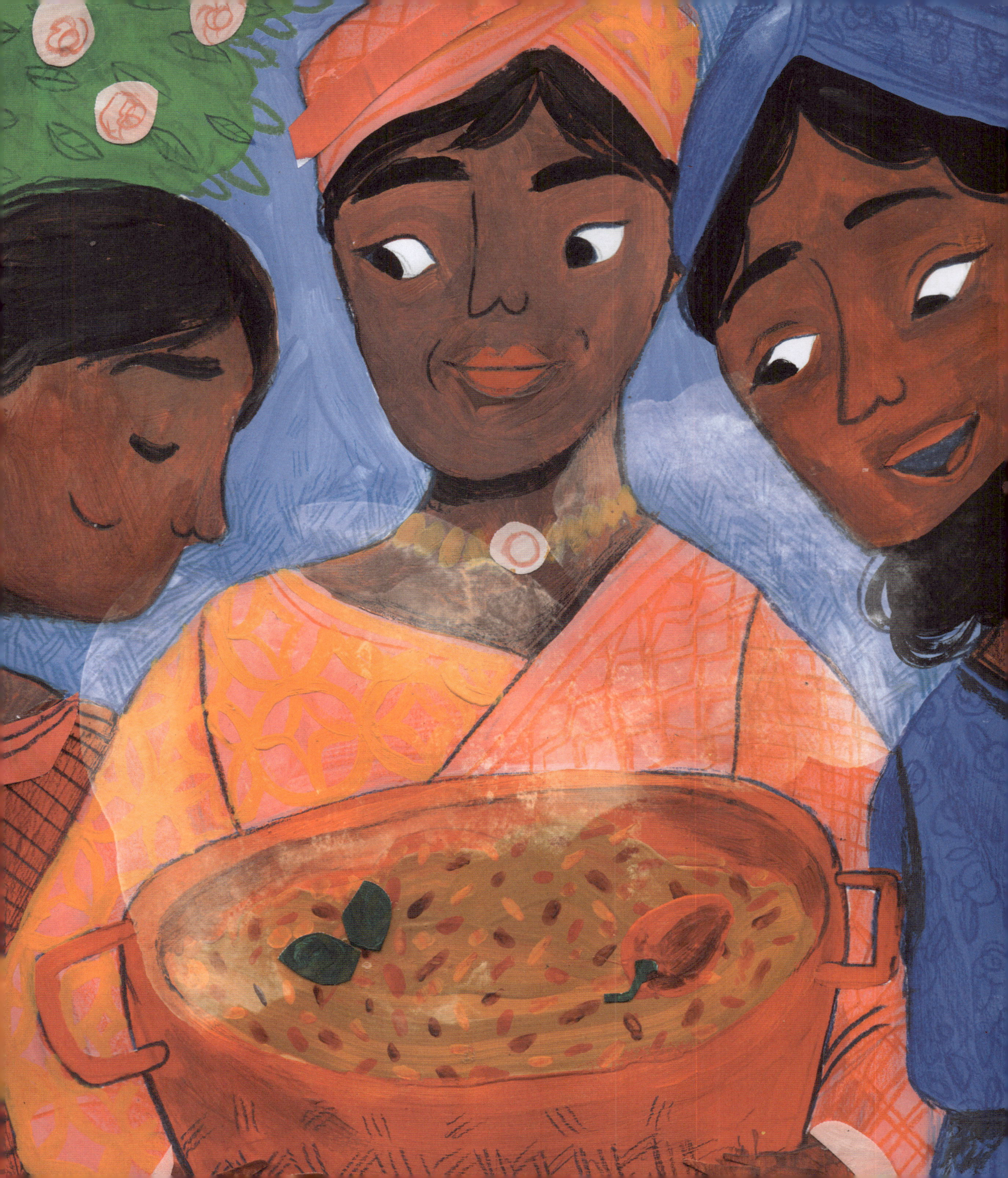

ancient Wolof empire that was once part of the country of Senegal, hence the name 'jollof', which is believed to be a variation of the word 'Wolof'. Confusingly though, the Senegalese call it ceebu jën, and typically serve the dish with fish and vegetables including aubergine, white cabbage, cassava, sweet potato and okra.

Claim that your country invented Jollof rice and you get a debate almost as hot as the dish itself. What everyone does agree on is its status as a beloved culinary treasure in West Africa and beyond!

WHY ICE CREAM CONES ARE BETTER FOR US THAN PENNY LICKS

If there is a single thing that unites all people, everywhere, it's that we love to eat things that are sweet and cold! From ancient China where natural ice was mixed with literal cream, to Alaskans using their naturally cold environment, to people from Iran defying the heat of the desert with yakhchals (buildings that were engineered to work like giant refrigerators) . . . we love ice cream.

Penny Lick

Although ice cream began with mixing ice and cream thousands of years ago, the waffle cone is pretty new. In fact, one of the ways we would eat ice cream was from a glass! In the early 1900s, ice cream was served in penny licks. They were pretty little glasses that cost a penny when filled with ice cream, with people licking the glass clean and tasting every last morsel!

Afterwards, the glasses were washed, of course. But still there were scary diseases going around that could be spread easily. Doctors warned others about buying penny licks, so they wouldn't get sick as well. It helped that the ice cream cone and waffle cone had been recently invented. It's hard to stop people from eating ice cream, but when you offer it in a cone you can eat, you have a winner for the ages!

WHY THERE IS A PINEAPPLE HOUSE IN SCOTLAND

In the 1500s in a place called Guadeloupe, the explorer Christopher Columbus, and those who travelled with him, made an exciting discovery. Among all the fresh fruits and vegetables, they found a strange and delicious fruit that looked like a pinecone but tasted as sweet as an apple . . . They thought it was amazing and decided to take it back to Spain.

It was hard to keep food fresh throughout long ship voyages – but the pineapple made it across the ocean. You can imagine that in 16th-century England, finding a sweet and unique fruit like this was rare! So the pineapple became very special: it was a distinctive and delightful treat that everyone wanted. It was so valuable that it was worth 8000 British pounds in today's money. People would show off a pineapple at parties as a way to flaunt how rich they were. And after the party, an even richer person would get to eat it.

In a place called Airth, Scotland, there was a man named John Murray, the fourth Earl of Dunmore. He had been the last English governor of Virginia but returned to Scotland in 1776. He wanted to show off his wealth, so he came up with a big idea. He built a huge pineapple structure on the roof of his house – it was a whopping 13.7 metres tall! This giant pineapple house became a symbol of his rich lifestyle.

And that's the story of how the pineapple travelled from Guadeloupe to inspire a grand pineapple house in Scotland. It reminds us of how much people loved and admired this extraordinary fruit for many hundreds of years.

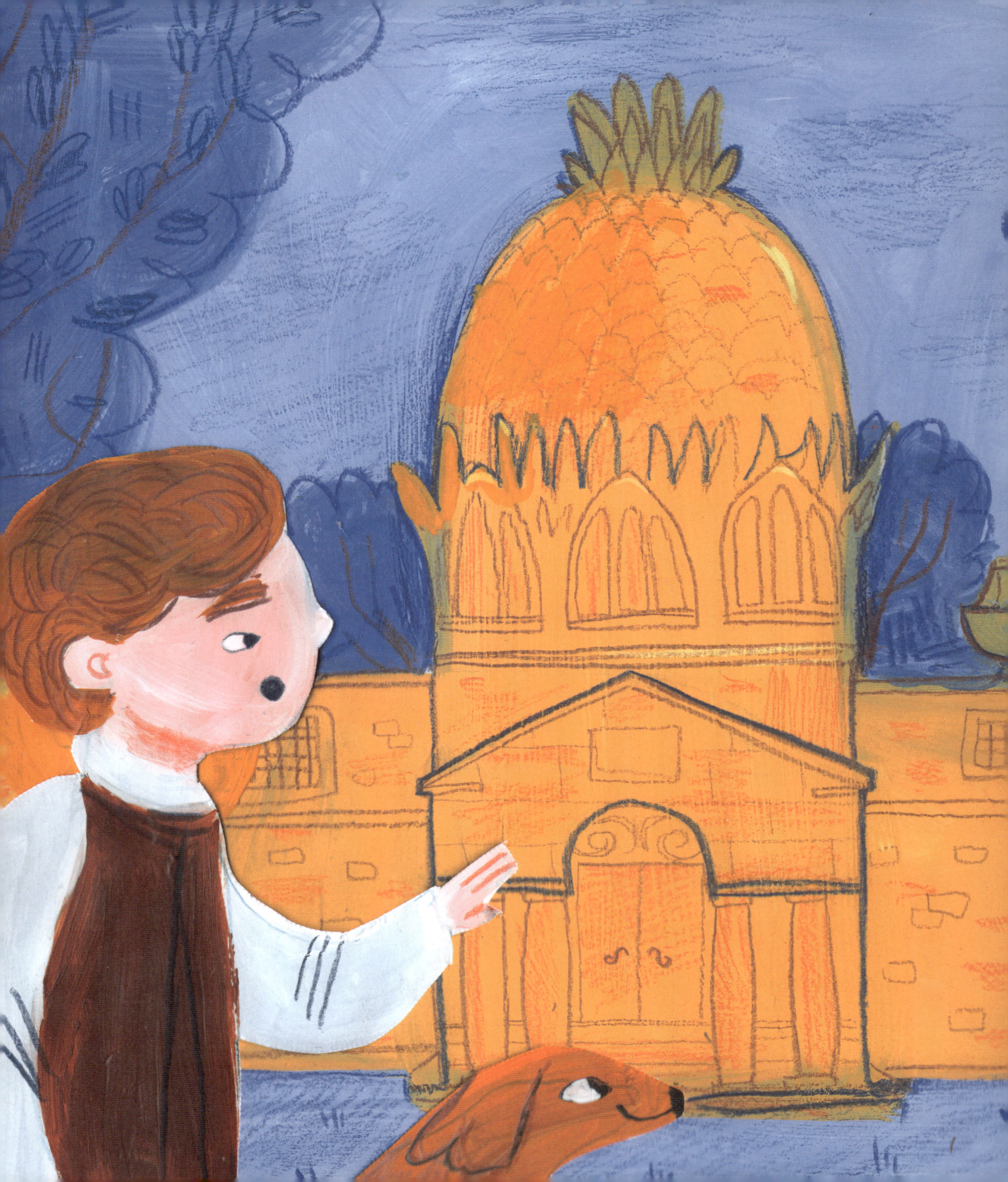

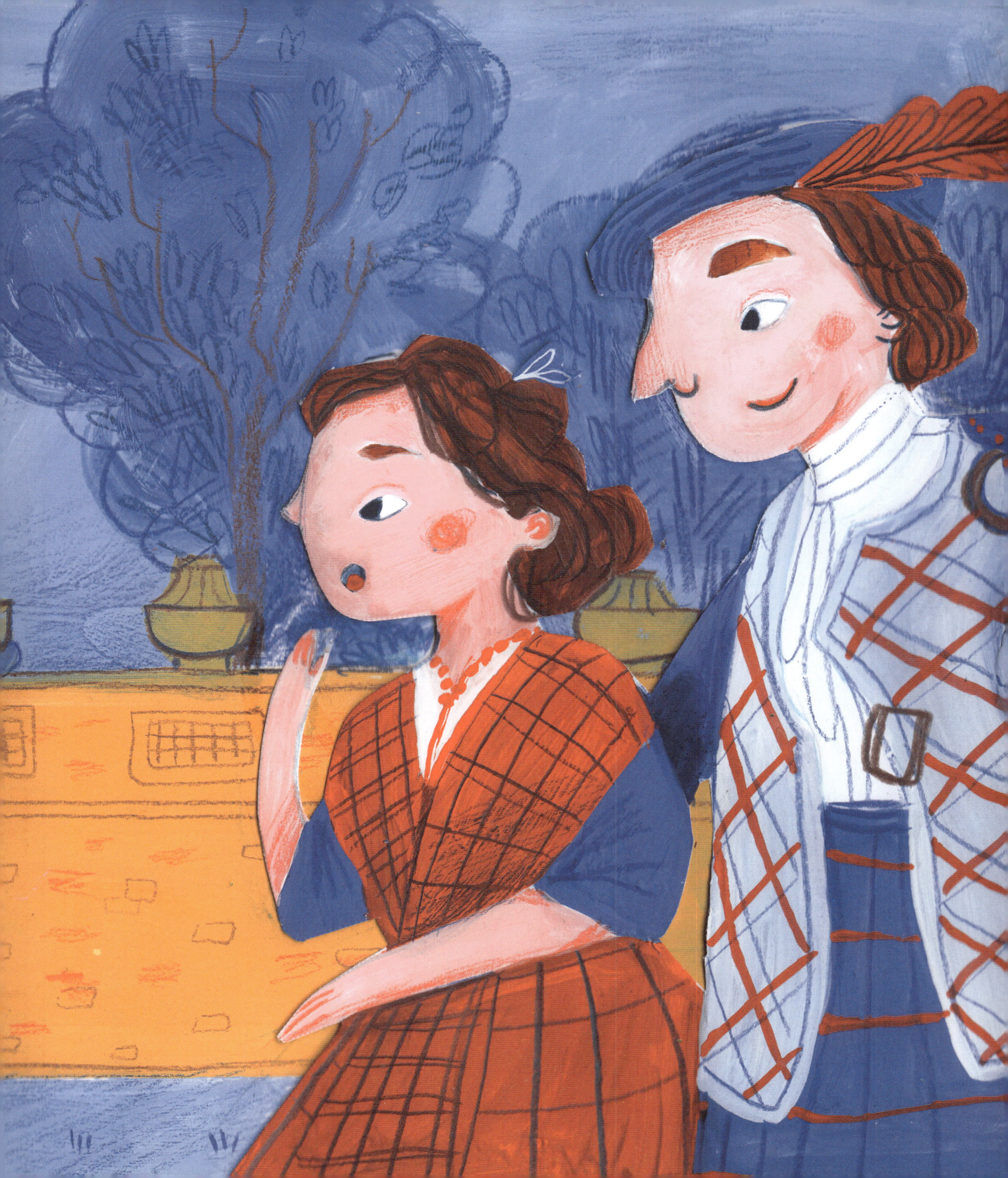

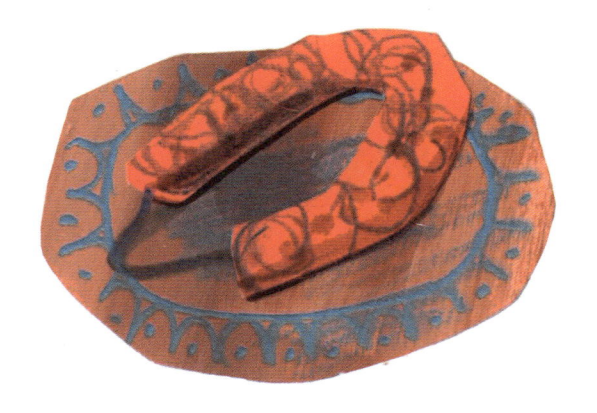

WHEN A SNEAKY SAUSAGE SAVED JEWISH PEOPLE IN PORTUGAL

Long ago, in the 16th century, the Spanish Inquisition spread to Portugal, which meant the beginning of a scary time for people who followed the Jewish faith.

The rulers at that time were part of the Inquisition, which didn't like Jewish people and treated them very badly. They were hunted, sent away from their homes, and some were even killed.

Being Jewish and practicing their religion became dangerous. There were spies everywhere, always watching what others were doing.

They would report on any signs of Jewish prayers or customs. Even the way they cooked their food was noticed, such as if they didn't hang up their sausages to dry. This was the usual way of preserving food to be eaten much later, but most sausages were made with ingredients that Jewish people don't eat because of their religion. So if a family didn't hang any up it was an easy way to tell they were Jewish.

But the clever Jewish people in the city of Mirandela came up with a plan. They created a special sausage called 'alheira'. It looked just like a regular pork sausage, but it was actually made with poultry and bread. This tricked the authorities into thinking they were eating pork. Hanging this sausage in their homes, no one could tell if they were secretly still practicing the Jewish customs.

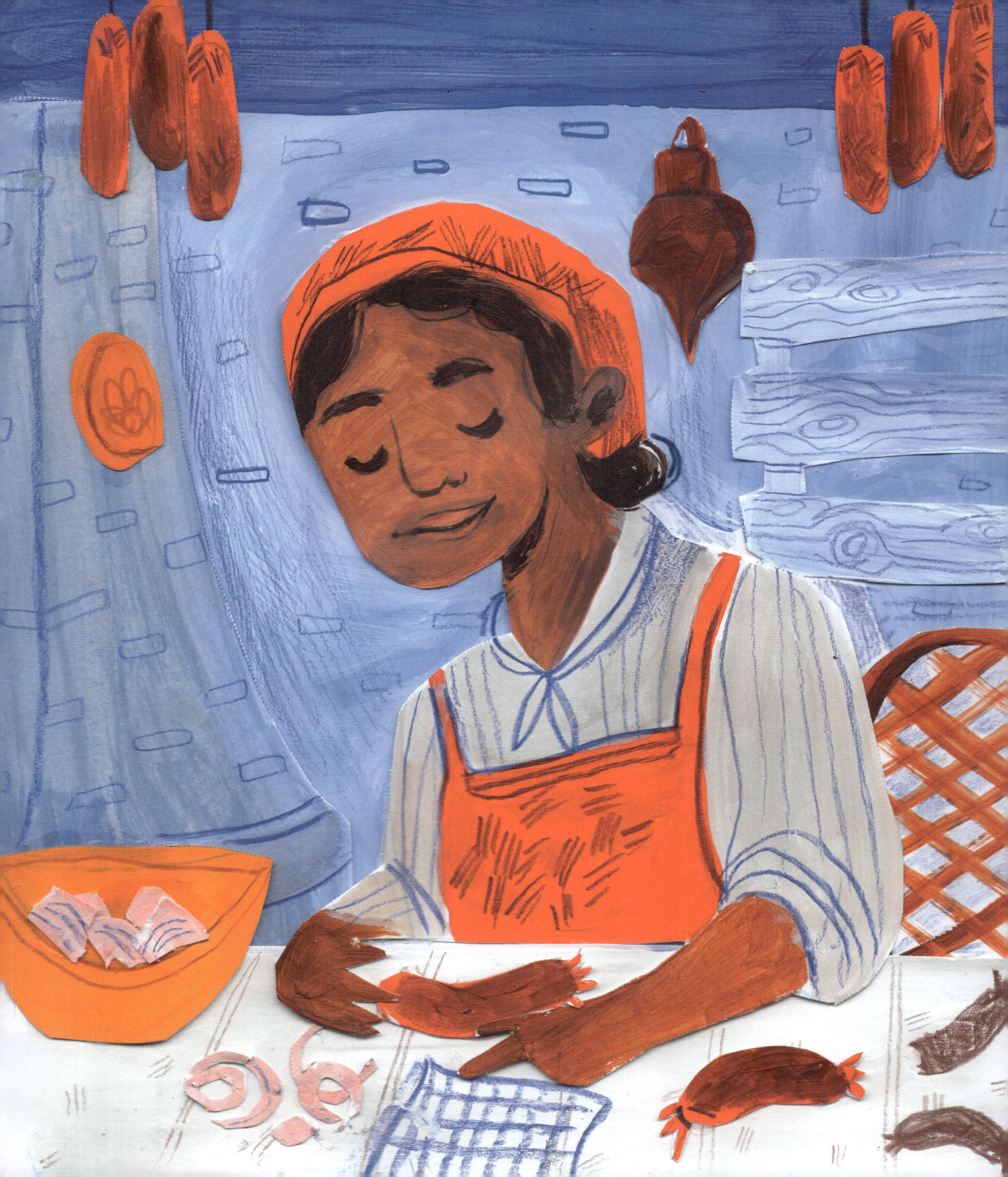

Today, people still eat alheira sausage, but many have forgotten its true story: it's a reminder of the brave Jewish people who found a clever way to keep their faith during those difficult times.

HOW A MUSTARD ARMY SPICED UP DIJON'S IMAGE

Long ago, in Ancient Greece, Rome and China, people already knew about mustard. It was famous and loved for a very long time before our story begins. In the 14th century, the Dukes of Burgundy, who were important people, liked mustard and celebrated it. But making mustard was expensive and not easy, which of course is why it was a big deal!

In Dijon, a city in Burgundy, a special mustard was made in closely controlled conditions. If anyone made bad mustard, they had to pay a lot of money as a punishment.

In 1383, Charles VI, the King of France, asked Philip the Bold, the Duke of Burgundy, for help. The Count of Flanders needed rescuing. So, Philip gathered an army of 1000 men. But how would they pay for it? Philip had a clever idea. He decided to ask for a donation in the form of a small coin, worth 10 cents, from the powerful mustard merchants.

Philip's army fought and won the battle to set the Count of Flanders free. On their way back to Dijon, Philip said, 'Moult me tarde de rentrer à Dijon', which meant he couldn't wait to get back to Dijon. They embroidered those words on their flag.

But when they arrived in Dijon, the wind made the flag move, and the fold covered parts of the sentence. People from far away saw the flag and thought it said, 'The mustard maker army is arriving'!

The people of Dijon were happy and excited, and took pride in the help of the mustard makers! In honour of this

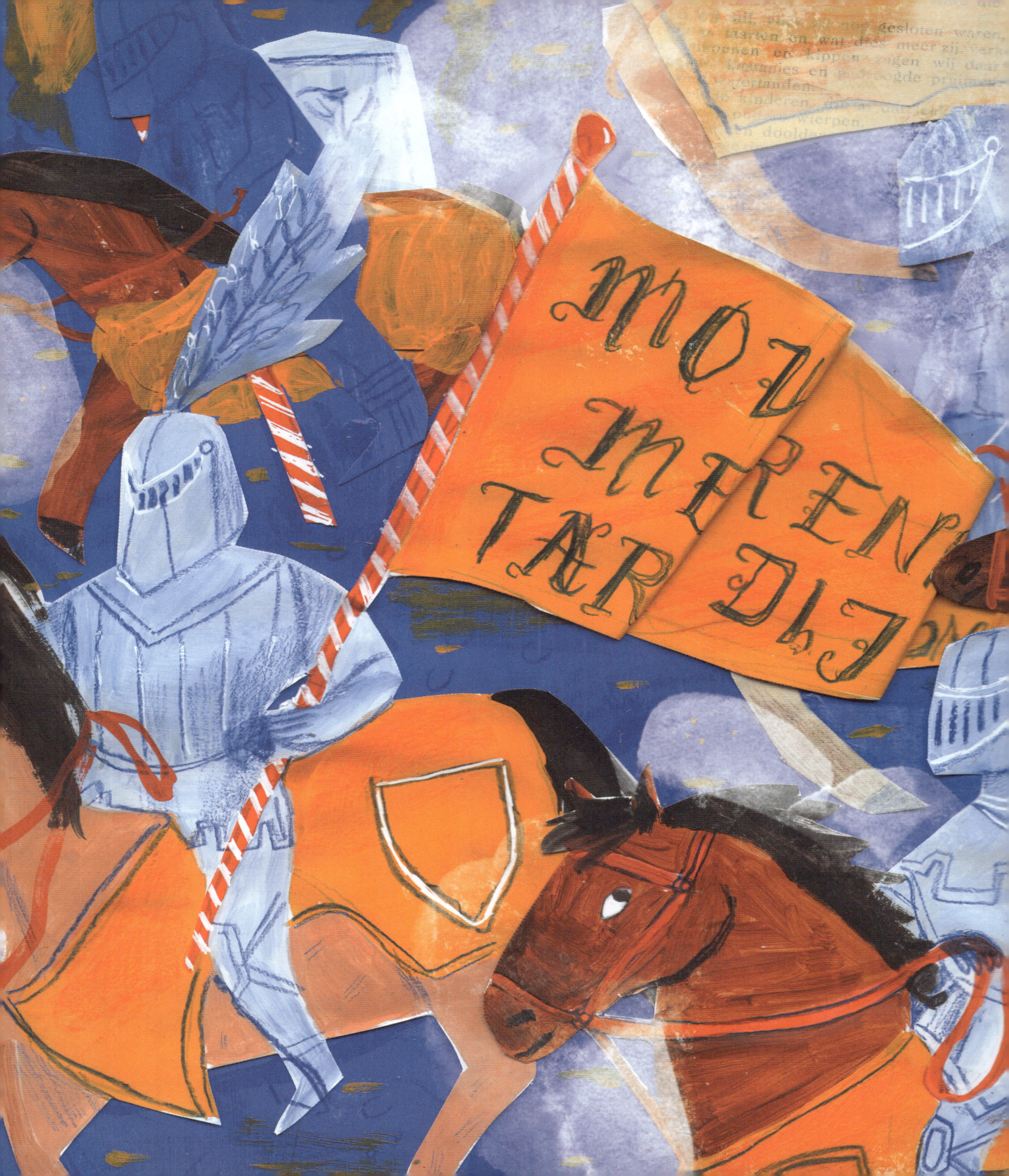

funny mistake, Philip allowed the mustard producers to be called mustard makers and use the Burgundy coat of arms on their mustard.

So, the next time you dip something into mustard, think about this story. Imagine if there really was a mustard army. Would you be afraid?

WHEN A MASH BECAME A SYMBOL FOR VICTORY

In the winter months, the Dutch people gather to eat a specific hearty dish called hutspot. It's a mash of potato, carrot and onion, usually eaten with sausage. Sounds pretty average, right? But do you know how it all began?

Legend has it that a young boy named Cornelis played a part in its discovery, at the end of the Dutch war with Spain in 1574.

For many months, the Spanish army had been camped just

outside the walls of Cornelis's home city, Leiden, in the Netherlands, fighting battles with Dutch rebels, and not allowing anyone (or anything, including food) to get in or out.

Growing desperate with the lack of food, the Dutch government voted to open surrounding dykes to flood the land. The Dutch rebels grew fierce, used small boats to fight, and the Spaniards fled.

On 3 October 1574, Cornelis walked beyond his city walls for the first time in many months, to find a deserted camp. He stumbled upon a remarkable find – a cooking pot filled with carrots, onions, meat and potato. Hungry and curious, Cornelis tasted the delicious mixture. It was a hearty and comforting meal.

Word spread about this discovery after things had settled, and people began calling it hutspot. The dish became associated with the event known as Het Leids Ontzet – the liberation of Leiden.

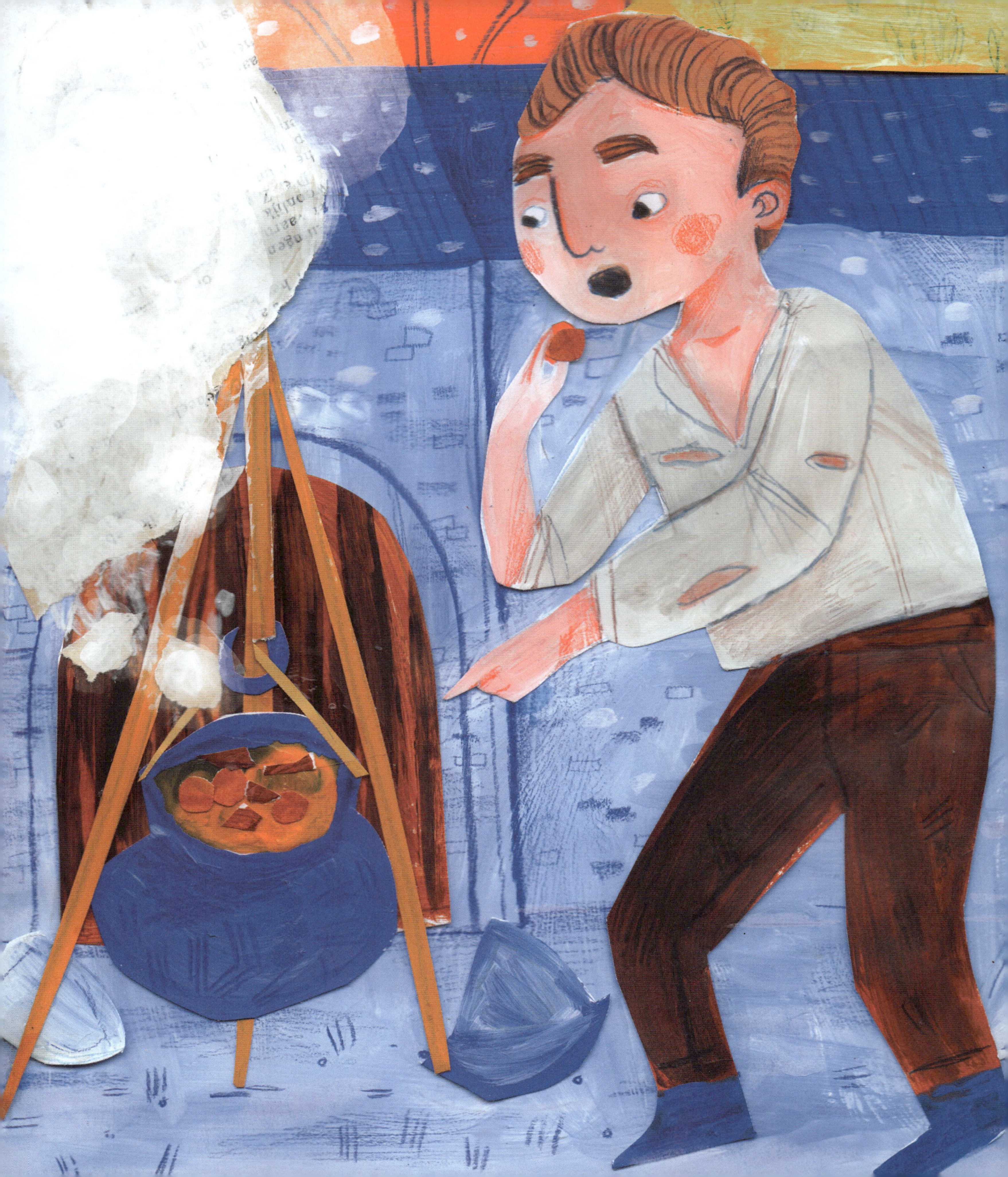

To this day, on 3 October, the people of Leiden come together to commemorate their city's freedom by enjoying a plate of hutspot. It is a reminder of Cornelis's adventure and the resilience of their community during challenging times. So, when you savour a bite of hutspot, remember the brave boy who stumbled upon this tasty tradition.

AUTHOR'S NOTE

Hey there, reader!

I hope you've enjoyed this tasty journey through the exciting world of food history! In this book, we've explored the stories, cultures and connections behind some of the exciting ingredients and yummy dishes we love. Food isn't just about filling our tummies; it's like a beautiful tapestry made with love, creativity and teamwork.

Throughout history, people have valued and protected their special recipes and food traditions – through the good and bad. Some were forced to be away from their homeland and had their freedom taken away, or had to fight invaders; others went elsewhere for marriage or just got creative with what they had.

It makes sense because food is a big part of our cultures, and something that we want to keep safe. But sometimes, this can make it hard for new flavours and ideas to be introduced and for different cultures to work together and make something awesome.

In our adventure, we've celebrated how amazing food is and the incredible stories it tells. It's not just about finding out who made a dish first; it's about understanding what it means and where it came from. Food is like a cultural ambassador that brings traditions, memories and values from all around the world. If you'd like to learn more about food culture and food traditions, there is a section after this called 'Bibliography' that you might like.

We have also explored how food cultures can travel and become a part of people's lives in different countries. It's amazing how dishes we usually think belong to one place can become popular and loved in faraway lands, or even had their origins in unexpected places. It shows how connected we all are and how food can bring us together, no matter where we're from.

The aim of this book is to bring people closer, to make you curious and excited about trying new flavours and experiencing different cultures through their food. It's not about knowing the exact history; it's about the messages and experiences that each dish brings. By sharing these stories, I hope to help you appreciate the awesome variety of food that makes our world so delicious.

I hope you're now readier than ever to enjoy everything the world has to offer with an open mind and a healthy appetite! Let's celebrate the amazing language of food and enjoy the shared experiences it brings. Bon appétit!

Yours hungrily,
Anna Lena

Find out more about Anna Lena:
www.annalena.nl | @annalenavaniersel

USING THE RECIPES

If you're anything like me, you'll be hungry after reading this book! I wanted to try some of these recipes and I was interested in how, when we make them for ourselves, we add our own flavour to them. Have a look at my website for inspiration on some of these recipes, and how to make them your own. If you make any of these recipes, please ask your grown-up to help and to confirm that you don't have an allergy to any of the ingredients. If you want to try experimenting with your own choice of ingredients, have fun, but make sure you check with a grown-up! Happy cooking!

www.annalena.nl/tastytales

BIBLIOGRAPHY: THE RECIPE FOR THIS BOOK

You might like to know where the information that shapes all these stories comes from! Below you will find it bundled into a *bibliography*, which is a list of sources that are used to write a book like this. Kind of like a recipe! To make this book, I have used . . .

A pinch of books . . .
- Allen, Stewart Lee, *In the Devil's Garden: A Sinful History of Forbidden Food* (Ballantine Books, 2003)
- Claiborne, Craig, *Craig Claiborne's The New York Times Food Encyclopedia* (Times Books, 1985: p.178)
- Dalby, Andrew, *Dangerous Tastes: The Story of Spices* (University of California Press, 2000: pp.133–4)
- Davidson, Alan, *The Oxford Companion to Food* (Oxford University Press, 1999: pp788–9)
- Mariani, John F, *Encyclopedia of American Food and Drink* (Lebhar Friedman, 1999: p.114)
- Pettigrew, Jane, *A Social History of Tea* (The National Trust, 2001: pp.102–105)
- Schrecker, Ellen and John Shrecker, *Mrs. Chiang's Szechwan Cookbook* (Harper & Row, 1976: p.220)
- Wilson, Bee, *Consider the Fork, A History of How We Cook and Eat* (Basic Books, 2013)
- Wong, Cecily and Dylan Thuras, *Gastro Obscura* (Workman, 2021)

A sprinkle of websites . . .
- Atlas Obscura – Articles on hot chocolate, the penny lick and more:
  www.atlasobscura.com/articles/who-invented-hot-chocolate
  www.atlasobscura.com/foods/penny-lick-ice-cream
- Coffee Prices – Kaldi's discovery: www.coffee-prices.com/how-did-kaldi-stumble-upon-the-coffee-plant/
- Comme Des Francais – Origins of tarte tatin: commedesfrancais.com/gb/story/tatin-tarte-dessert
- Culture Trip – Brief histories on dulce de leche, jollof rice and more:
  theculturetrip.com/south-america/uruguay/articles/a-brief-history-of-dulce-de-leche
  theculturetrip.com/africa/ghana/articles/a-brief-history-of-jollof-rice-a-west-african-favourite
- Farmers Almanac – The unusual history of the potato:
  www.farmersalmanac.com/parmentier-made-potatoes-popular-28537
- Food Timeline – Articles on cotton candy, nachos, gingerbread and more:
  www.foodtimeline.org/foodcandy.html#cottoncandy
  www.foodtimeline.org/foodmexican.html#nachos
  www.foodtimeline.org/christmasfood.html#gingerbread
- Free Heri Heri for All: www.freeheriheriforall.com/
- GOYA – A story of petha: www.goya.in/blog/petha-a-confection-as-old-as-the-taj-mahal

- HistoryHit – The Earl of Sandwich:
www.historyhit.com/did-the-4th-earl-of-sandwich-really-invent-the-sandwich/
- Historic UK – Origins of pancake day: www.historic-uk.com/CultureUK/Pancake-Day/
- Historiek (Dutch-language site) – The importance of hutspot: historiek.net/leidens-ontzet-1574-hutspot-haring-wittebrood/83457/#:~:text=Hutspot%20en%20het%20Leidens%20Ontzet&text=In%20het%20verlaten%20legerkamp%20zou,met%20klapstuk
- Lemelson MIT – Discussion of instant noodles: lemelson.mit.edu/resources/momofuku-ando
- Pomona College – All about okra:
www.pomona.edu/farm/blog/posts/okra-how-it-got-united-states-how-grow-it-and-how-eat-it
- Thai Ginger – A story of pad thai:
thaiginger.com/the-history-of-pad-thai-how-the-amazing-dish-came-to-be/
- Vice – Article on Om Ali: amuse.vice.com/en_us/article/a3p874/om-ali-egyptian-dessert

If you are still hungry for more, you can find suggestions for further reading on my website, along with the recipe ideas to try. There are some wonderful old cookery books and food history resources to discover, and fascinating articles on the websites of, among others, the United Nations and the British Library.

Disclaimer: The websites listed in the endmatter of this book are the property of their respective owners. UCLan Publishing and the University of Central Lancashire do not control the websites listed and identified in this book and expressly disclaims any responsibility for the content, the accuracy of the information and any products or services available on those websites. If you decide to access or engage in services through the linked websites, you do so at your own risk. You should direct any concerns regarding any websites to the administrator of the applicable websites. You should also refer to the separate terms of use, privacy policies and other rules posted on the websites before you use them. This book is a publication of UCLan Publishing and it has not been prepared, approved, endorsed or licensed by any other person or entity.

ACKNOWLEDGEMENTS

I want to thank all the sweet and talented people that made this book a reality: Hazel Holmes, with UCLan Publishing, for believing in *Tasty Tales* and being an overall delight. Nicki Marshall, my editor, for her smart and thoughtful suggestions and nice chats. Becky Chilcott, talented designer, for making this book more pretty than I could have imagined. A special thanks to my agent, Christabel McKinley, for representing me straight towards having my dream project published. I'm very lucky to work with you!

Thanks to Monique and Wim, my mother and father, for always encouraging me to make the most of life, and for sharing their love of books with me. Thank you also for taking great care of Floris while I work on my books. Thank you to the Gouda gang for being so creative in your own ways, and inspiring me – you are absolute nerds. And finally: thanks to my beautiful husband and son, Robbert and Floris, for being my home.